TOP
JOBS

TOP
JOBS

HOW THEY ARE DIFFERENT
AND WHAT YOU NEED TO SUCCEED

KEVIN KELLY

Vice President, Publisher: Tim Moore
Associate Publisher and Director of Marketing: Amy Neidlinger
Acquisitions Editor: Jennifer Simon
Editorial Assistant: Heather Luciano
Development Editor: Russ Hall
Operations Manager: Gina Kanouse
Digital Marketing Manager: Julie Phifer
Publicity Manager: Laura Czaja
Assistant Marketing Manager: Megan Colvin
Cover Designer: Chuti Prasertsith
Managing Editor: Kristy Hart
Project Editor: Betsy Harris
Copy Editor: Krista Hansing
Proofreader: Language Logistics
Compositor: Jake McFarland
Manufacturing Buyer: Dan Uhrig

FT Press offers excellent discounts on this book when ordered in quantity for bulk purchases or special sales. For more information, please contact U.S. Corporate and Government Sales, 1-800-382-3419, corpsales@pearsontechgroup.com. For sales outside the U.S., please contact International Sales at international@pearson.com.

Company and product names mentioned herein are the trademarks or registered trademarks of their respective owners.

Printed in the United States of America

First Printing February 2009

ISBN-10: 0-13-712781-2
ISBN-13: 978-0-13-712781-8

Pearson Education LTD.
Pearson Education Australia PTY, Limited.
Pearson Education Singapore, Pte. Ltd.
Pearson Education North Asia, Ltd.
Pearson Education Canada, Ltd.
Pearson Educatión de Mexico, S.A. de C.V.
Pearson Education—Japan
Pearson Education Malaysia, Pte. Ltd.

Library of Congress Cataloging-in-Publication Data

Kelly, Kevin.

   Top jobs : how they are different and what you need to succeed / Kevin Kelly.

      p. cm.

   ISBN 0-13-712781-2 (hardback : alk. paper) 1. Chief executive officers. 2. Career development. 3. Success in business. 4. Leadership. I. Title.

   HD38.2.K4664 2009

   658.4'09—dc22

                              2008019932

To my parents

Contents

Acknowledgments

I would like to thank all those leaders who found time in their schedules to talk to me about their own top jobs. In particular, thanks are due to the following:

Jacques Aigrain, CEO, Swiss Re, Switzerland

Richard Baker, CEO, Alliance Boots, UK

Carlos Ghosn, president and CEO, Nissan, Japan; president and CEO, Renault, France

Tim Flynn, chairman, KPMG International and chairman and CEO, KPMG LLP, United States

Rick Goings, chairman and CEO, Tupperware Brands Corporation; chairman, Boys and Girls Clubs of America

Seung-Yu Kim, CEO, Hana Financial Group, Korea

Gary Knell, president and CEO, Sesame Workshop, United States

Bruno Lafont, chairman and CEO, Lafarge, France

Chip McClure, chairman, CEO, and president, ArvinMeritor, United States

Takeshi Niinami, president and CEO, Lawson, Japan

James Owens, chairman and CEO, Caterpillar, United States

Monika Ribar, president and CEO, Panalpina, Switzerland

Stuart Rose, CEO, Marks & Spencer, UK

Carl Schramm, president and CEO, Kaufmann Foundation, United States

Peter Sharpe, President and CEO of Cadillac Fairview Corporation

James Skinner, vice chairman and CEO, McDonald's, United States

H. Patrick Swygert, president of Howard University, United States

The senior chairman of Heidrick & Struggles, Gerry Roche, was also kind enough to lend me insights from his legendary career in search. Gerry has probably recruited more business leaders than anyone else in the world, and I am very grateful for his time.

Steve Tappin of Heidrick & Struggles provided great comment on his own extensive research into CEOs in the UK.

My thanks to Heidrick & Struggles board members Richard Beattie (Simpson Thacher & Bartlett) and Jill Kanin-Lovers, who both offered invaluable assistance.

To Stuart Crainer, without whom the writing of this book would not have been possible.

To my publishers Liz Gooster and Jennifer Simon for all their good advice, and to Narda Shirley and Tashi Lassalle for their inspirations and creative support in turning this book from an idea into a reality.

The support and hard work of Jacqueline Wilson and Claire Davies made this task a whole lot easier.

Thanks to David Peters for his eagle-eyed proofing.

Inhye Kim, Bernard Zen-Ruffinen, Grace Moon, Fran Minogue, Nathaniel J. Sutton, Rob Hines, Torrey Foster, Dale Visokey, and John Gardner for finding time to help me set up interviews with the leaders. And Preeti Seshadri for her research help.

My wife Michele for her love, support, and, most of all, her patience, particularly when it comes to replacing light bulbs.

To all my great colleagues at Heidrick & Struggles.

…and to my friend Sam.

About the Author

Kevin Kelly was named Chief Executive Officer of the world's leading headhunting firm, Heidrick & Struggles, in September 2006.

One of a new generation of global CEOs, Kelly regularly contributes to public debate on the nature of leadership today, with particular insights into cross-cultural subtleties, leveraging technology and social network.

With a decade's experience in Tokyo, Kelly spent three years in London running Heidrick & Struggles EMEA operations before returning to his native America to lead the $650 million company.

Named Headhunter of the Year in 2000 by Finance Intelligence Asia, and "One of Asia's Top Recruiters" four years running by *Asia-Money* magazine, Kelly has extensive first-hand experience building senior leadership teams for the word's most successful companies.

This personal experience with clients informs his view on what it takes to lead a global company in the twenty-first century.

He believes passionately that culture drives commercial success.

Kelly holds a bachelor's degree from George Mason University in Fairfax, Virginia, and an MBA from Duke University's Fuqua School of Business, where he serves on the Board of Visitors.

Introduction

This book began with a question: "What does it take to survive and succeed in a top job?"

Working in executive search the world over, from Boston to Beijing, from Seattle to Sao Paolo, this question has followed me from client meeting to client meeting. How do talented individuals succeed or fail in the top job? What is the leap in mindset and mentality that comes with the corner office? How do you jump in? I thought from observation that I knew. Then in September 2006 came the real test that only I could answer, as I stepped into the ultimate top job—that of CEO.

It seemed the perfect time to address the issue with a new degree of seriousness.

What do you need to do to enjoy a top job?

What are the pressures?

What are the compensations?

Where are the pitfalls?

How do you avoid them?

And was I ever going to see my family again?

Working with some of the most demanding clients and talented individuals in business, I have witnessed the dizziest of successes and the deepest of failures. Now it was time for me to find out for myself what it meant to take the lead, to step up to the top job.

As Stephen Miles, a partner in Leadership Consulting at Heidrick & Struggles, said to me, "It's what you learn after you think you know everything that counts."

In my experience, most leaders fail because they think they know everything. I wanted to find the ones who knew better.

The leaders I have talked to are from all around the globe: Some are seasoned senior executives; others are newer to the job, like me.

But whatever their experience, common themes emerge. It doesn't matter which company they're in—the people issues, the communication issues, the complexities of compensation, finding time for family—they're the same for anyone in a truly top job.

Many of these questions mirror my own preoccupations: These are common dilemmas that arise every day.

The first is communication: how it can be misunderstood and how it should be handled.

The second is compensation: not just in a monetary sense but also in working to make every employee feel valued so they look forward to work each morning. Because it really all comes down to people, doesn't it? What is amazing to me is that we study business at university or business school and spend 95 percent of the time learning about strategy, marketing, corporate finance, organizational structure, and so on and about 5 percent on people skills. Yet, when we finish our studies and start working, we immediately find the opposite emphasis to be true. Personnel issues fill your days, whether you're working in an organization of ten or ten thousand. Day to day, every plan you make and every strategy you devise revolves around having the right people in place.

Change is another preoccupation. Charles Darwin said: "It is not the strongest of the species that survives, nor the most intelligent. It is the one that is the most adaptable to change."

Top leaders embrace change and bend to it. They drive it and are consumed by it. But how do you balance change with continuity? How do you keep your feet on the ground when all about you others are losing theirs? How do you become the master rather than the puppet of your corporate destiny?

These are just some of the questions that I faced taking on my own challenges, and I suspect these are the challenges you may someday face, or already face, also.

I must admit, writing this book has been therapeutic. I think I am a little closer to the truth. Leadership is lonely. I hope reading this you find some companionship and guidance as you yourself pursue your dream career, your top job. And I sincerely hope that reading *Top Jobs* is as helpful to you as the writing of it has been to me.

Kevin Kelly
Chicago
June 2008

1

Why Top Jobs Matter

The leaders of organizations are not decorative adornments. They make a real and lasting difference to how individuals and organizations perform.

> "It is a 24/7 thing. And while you're not necessarily at work, you're on call, and you're accountable for what's going on in your world. We've got 100,000 people. Literally, somebody is working on Caterpillar business all the time, every day, somewhere in the world. You just get used to that."
>
> —*Jim Owens, chairman and CEO, Caterpillar*

A Day in a Top Job

5:45 a.m.: My wife is out of town. I get up and go for a run. I think while I run. Most leaders I talk to do something like this, whether it's playing tennis or going to the gym. I then get my four kids (ages 10, 8, 6, and 4) up and dressed, get me dressed, get them to the bus stop, and get me to the train station.

7:45 a.m.: Call the Shanghai office to check in, scan my emails on the train, and then jump into a cab and make calls until I arrive at the office at 8:15, when I have a 15-minute catch-up with my executive assistant.

8:30 a.m.: Speak to our chief financial officer for Asia–Pacific, who is based out of Sydney.

9:00 a.m.: Talk to one of our U.K.–based consultants about the successes of a new private equity initiative the firm is working on.

9:30 a.m.: Meet with human resources about a couple key new hires in Europe.

10:30 a.m.: Prepare for the upcoming board meeting with the director of communications.

11:30 a.m.: Meet with three of our top-billing consultants.

12:15 p.m.: Lunch with the head of the World Economic Forum, Karl Schwab, to discuss a new joint initiative with Heidrick & Struggles.

1:30–2:30 p.m.: Hold a 360-degree review with external coach/consultant as part of the work we're doing realigning our leadership team.

2:30 p.m.: Call our office managing partner in Paris.

3:00 p.m.: Squeeze in a meeting with a U.S. consultant on a last-minute trip to the London office.

3:30 p.m.: Meet to discuss the strategic reorganization of our practices in North America.

4:30 p.m.: Meet with Stuart Rose, CEO of Marks & Spencer.

5:45 p.m.: Call our CFO.

6:00 p.m.: Call the external consulting firm that is reviewing the Heidrick & Struggles business model.

6:30 p.m.: Call a partner in São Paulo, Brazil, and then another in Encino.

7:00 p.m.: Call company senior chairman Gerry Roche from a cab on the way to the station. Then check more emails while I'm on the train.

8:00 p.m.: Arrive home. My daughter tells me she needs help with her homework on prisms. I have to eat my dinner, get the three younger children to bed and read their bedtime stories, and figure out what a prism is.

9:00–10:45 p.m.: Participate in an Executive Committee call.

10:46 p.m.: Answer a call from the head of Asia–Pacific asking for a couple extra minutes. I say, "Can we talk tomorrow morning?" He says "Fine, sure," but we still end up chatting.

And suddenly it's 11:20 p.m., and I hit the pillow until the alarm goes off at 5:45 again.

People often ask me how I spend my time. That was a pretty typical day when I worked from our London office (I have since relocated to Chicago). The rest of the time I am on the road. The reality is that every time I am on the move, I make a call; every time I have a break, I call someone. I go through a mental list of who I haven't spoken to for a while or someone I know who has a new piece of work or who has family news—perhaps a new baby or something.

Why do I tell you all this? Because life in a top job is not for everyone. It is a grueling, stressful, and often lonely existence. I want you to know that up front, before you get involved or before you start dreaming of being a leader. I want you to know that it is physically, mentally, and emotionally demanding. And, of course, there is no guarantee of success or even survival in the post. So why do it? Because, on a good day, it is also the best job in the world.

Making a Difference

A top job in a modern organization is a serious, time-consuming, tiring, demanding, exciting, and rewarding experience. At the top, there are no half-measures. You don't climb half a mountain. You don't take in half a view. You don't address half an audience. You can't run any significant organization, part of an organization, or team of people unless you are prepared to give enormous and whole-hearted commitment. "I can't do the job halfway," one executive in a top job told me. "This is a do-it-all-the-way-or-step-aside-and-let-someone-else-do-it job. A lot of people wouldn't be willing to do that. On the other hand, there's no shortage of people who want to take on the challenge. By the time you get to the executive office, there are a lot people who've dropped out along the way, who've said, 'Hey, I'm not willing to move around the world, I'm not willing to make the kind of time commitments to this.'"

A top job demands total dedication and belief. This was brought home to me talking to Jim Skinner, CEO of McDonald's. When Skinner became CEO, he was the company's third leader in seven months, after Jim Cantalupo and Charlie Bell. He brought with him the dedication and enthusiasm of a true believer. "If you can't believe in your brand, you can't do your job with enthusiasm," Skinner says. "I believe strongly you work for your company; you don't work for the boss. And I always felt that paid great dividends in McDonald's, in terms of not only my ability to contribute, but also the support I received from the leadership of the organization—or, as our former chairman used to say, 'If we all agree all the time, then we don't need one of us.' I love the company—what it stands for, what we mean to the public, what we're responsible for, and what we're accountable for delivering."

Meeting up with someone like Skinner is reassuring. His commitment and belief is infectious. As you will see in this book, the lure of a top job is not about money. It's about changing things. It's about making a mark. It's about stewardship. It's about testing yourself in a leadership role.

As I discovered in my voyage around top jobs, sometimes a small idea seeded by a leader can have an immediate impact. Keeping up-to-date with fashion trends, Stuart Rose, CEO of the U.K. retailer Marks & Spencer (M&S), was leafing through *Vogue* when some shoes caught his eye. The next day, he went into the footwear department and asked why M&S didn't have similar style shoes in its range. The next afternoon, the head of operations for footwear let Rose know that the shoes had been designed and the factory in China was ready to begin production. The shoes arrived ten days later. "I used him a lot as an example at the time," says Rose. "It was about showing people this is a problem we can solve. A couple of youngsters were suddenly starting to say, 'Stuart, by the way, I've done this.' It was sort of exponential. One guy did something I made an example of, then another guy wanted to see if he could do that, then a couple more. Steve Rowe in household goods is a very aggressive trader, and he began slashing the prices. We used to sell a towel rail for £21 or £22; the same towel rails of the same quality are now £9.50. That's in the space of 24 months, and we're selling tens of thousands."

In any top job, your duty is to plant the seeds of tomorrow's value.

Magic Moments

The starting point for any top job is a moment with the potential to change the course of events—to change a team, a department, a division, an entire organization—and to alter the paths of careers and shape lives. These critical, path-shaping moments arrive when a new leader is appointed. Time stands still. The organization and its individuals are held up to blinding scrutiny. What they stand for, what they aspire to be, and how they intend to get there are appraised from every angle.

The pressure is intense for those charged with hiring and firing. If they get it right, they're heroes. "The number one responsibility of any public company's board is the succession planning and the hiring of the CEO," says Skinner. "Obviously, they have other governance responsibilities and shareholder responsibilities, but that's really their number one job. When they get that right, all other things sort of fall into place."

Such a moment was Jim McNerney's appointment as chairman and CEO of 3M. McNerney was fresh from the Jack Welch succession race at General Electric (GE), where Jeff Immelt had beaten him to the number 1 spot. Having worked across a broad range of GE business units, and with extensive international experience, including two years running GE's Asian operations, McNerney was considered a perfect fit with 3M.

Before the announcement, 3M's stock had been languishing in the $80–$90 range. On the day McNerney was hired, the stock jumped from $99 to $105 and reached a 52-week high of $122 within a month—all because McNerney was seen as a great choice.

After a slight hiccup at the outset, when he referred to 3M as GE at his first shareholders' meeting, McNerney brought some GE management science to bear on the wildfire innovation culture of 3M. He introduced Six Sigma, cut overheads, and created a leadership development institute along the lines of GE's Crotonville. At the same time, however, 3M's new CEO, the first outsider to lead the company, emphasized, "The story here is rejuvenation of a talented group of people rather than replacement of a mediocre group of people."

Between 1995 and 2000, shareholder returns at 3M had lagged behind the S&P 500. With McNerney at the helm, the shares climbed beyond the $120 mark, while the S&P 500 dipped by 30 percent.

No wonder, then, that Boeing's shares leaped 7 percent ($3.9 billion) and 3M's slumped 10 percent ($2.7 billion) on the 2005 announcement of McNerney's move out of 3M to the airplane manufacturer.

Share hikes inspired by new leaders are now common. On the 2005 announcement of Mark Hurd's joining Hewlett-Packard (HP) from NCR, HP's share price increased by 4 percent ($4.6 billion), and NCR's decreased by 5 percent ($0.6 billion). Research by Heidrick & Struggles in the United Kingdom covering 16 changes in CEOs within the FTSE 100 during 2005 found that the market value change on the announcement of a new CEO exceeds twice the daily fluctuation. Leadership makes a difference.

Getting It Wrong

Of course, there's always a flip side. A fumbled succession impacts not just staff morale and business performance, but a company's stock price as well. The early departure of the new leader can also cost a company a great deal in both severance pay and dented reputation.

Yet despite their best attentions, the issue continues to bedevil companies. Richard Thoman lasted a little more than a year as CEO of Xerox, from April 1999 to May 2000. During Thoman's brief watch, the market capitalization of Xerox fell by around $1 billion—that's 45 percent.

Other recent short-lived successions include Robert Nakasone, who became CEO of Toys R Us in 1998 but left just 18 months later. Nakasone saw Toys R Us plunged into disarray, overtaken by Wal-Mart as the biggest toy retailer in the United States. In a reverse of the new CEO stock boost effect, Toys R Us stock jumped 50¢ on the announcement of Nakasone's departure.

Gregory Wolf lasted less than two years as CEO of Humana. Under Wolf, Humana's stock lost more than half its value, a situation aggravated by a failed takeover of UnitedHealth Group (then known as United HealthCare Corp.).

Let's be clear: These leaders were bright people trying their best to succeed. When things go wrong, human factors usually appear to be the nub of the problem—and that goes for just about any appointment that doesn't work out. "I am certain that it's the selection process that's at fault, not the lack of forgiveness of the shareholders," says Warren Bennis, professor of business administration and founding chairman of the Leadership Institute at the University of Southern California. "Boards that go into rhapsodic overtures about leadership never really define what they mean by that word, nor do they pay enough attention to the human factor."

Most bungled successions can be traced to five all-too-human failings. First, many incumbent leaders are reluctant to give up the reins of power; either they hang on too long or they try to foist like-minded successors onto their boards. (You'll find the same thing going on at the school PTA committee or the kids' soccer league.) Second, boards tend to appoint a safe replacement instead of than someone who will question the role of those making the appointment. "Boards are rarely objective enough when recruiting leaders," one leader told me. Third, selection groups frequently fail to define or stick to an objective set of selection criteria, allowing themselves to be swayed by force of personality. Fourth, many don't look beyond the most visible candidates and, therefore, fail to identify potential leaders from the next generation of executives.

Finally, in too many cases, short-term concerns are allowed to dictate the succession timetable, with the decision driven by external pressures instead of business needs. Short-termism is a corporate virus. "The public markets bring an awful lot of pressure to a CEO of a public company; there is a somewhat selfish quest among investment managers to produce results to attract more clients," says Peter Sharpe, president and CEO of Cadillac Fairview Corporation, one of North America's largest commercial property firms. "I worry where the next great companies are going to come from. There's always such pressure to perform short-term, and very little patience with investment for the long-term benefit of, and growth of, the organization." Add to this the usual heady mix of executive egos, corporate politics, and greed, and you have a recipe for trouble.

When a company is performing well, succession problems tend to be a by-product of the success of the incumbent. M. Douglas Ivester, for instance, was ousted from the top job at Coca-Cola after a series of misjudgments. Professor Bennis surmises that the aura of his predecessor, Roberto Goizueta, dazzled the board into doing only a cursory vetting of his nominated successor. "Did the board really take a serious

look at his capacity to work with people, to thoroughly examine his relationship with his peers and direct reports? I doubt it," says Bennis.

Why Leaders Matter

The trials and tribulations of getting the right person in any top job
are clearly worth it. Consider the very top of the organization: the
CEO. As Jim McNerney shows, CEOs can make an incredible difference to an organization. Nitin Nohria and colleagues at Harvard Business School found that the leader accounts for 14 percent of a
company's performance (based on an examination of a group of companies that had an average of three CEOs over 24 years; figures
ranged as high as 40 percent for the hotels sector). Other research
found that nearly 50 percent of a company's reputation is linked to
CEO reputation (based on a survey of 1,155 business leaders in the
United States). Harvard's Rakesh Khurana estimates that anywhere
from 30 to 40 percent of the performance of a company is attributa-
ble to industry effects, 10 to 20 percent to cyclical economic changes,
and perhaps 10 percent to the CEO. Ten percent is still a great deal
for one individual to be responsible for.

Leaders matter—but let's get real, people in top jobs are not mir-
acle workers. They can't change things overnight or even in weeks or
months. It takes time. "When I took the job, I thought it was a five-
year project. That was a minimum expectation," says Richard Baker,
former CEO of the U.K. retail chain Alliance Boots. "It wasn't a quick
fix. Three years isn't long. You can't really change a culture in that
time, so five years is a reasonable yardstick."

The trouble is, time is often what leaders have least of. Top jobs
are not blessed with a great deal of security. Indeed, they are so pressured and insecure that it's remarkable people still want to take on
leadership roles. My suspicion is that people are now more skeptical

that the sacrifices inherent in top jobs are worth it. "CEOs are almost vilified in the press these days, and I'm sure that turns off a lot of people," says Cadillac Fairview Corporation's Peter Sharpe. "If you talk about being a president or a CEO to the average guy in the street, there's this little radar in the back of their mind that wonders whether the guy's just another greedy crook. I think younger people don't invest the same time in relationships that were expected 20 years ago. There really is a different attitude now. Business is going to get done, and they're going to accomplish it in different ways than we have."

I spoke at a conference for executives and asked those in the audience who wanted to be a CEO to raise their hand. Four hundred and fifty people sat in front of me. Four hands went up. Perhaps they all wanted to be CMOs or CFOs, but I suspect not. People increasingly are recognizing the price of leadership.

I told this story to Jim Owens, chairman and CEO of Caterpillar. He was skeptical of my skepticism. "I've got six group presidents. If you asked which one would like to have the opportunity to run the company, you'd probably have six hands go up," he said. "And if you ask the senior leadership teams at Alcoa or IBM, whose boards I'm on, I think a lot of hands would go up. But these are people who've been around the company for a long time; they understand it, they like it, and they're driven to be successful and to have the company be successful. So I do think it is a daunting task. I've been around the CEO, as a member of the executive office now, since 1995 and chairman since 2004. There is a step function increase, even if you're the number two guy, to being the number one guy. I was talking to my wife last night about going to a wedding. And I said, 'Well, I have to be back in Peoria on Sunday afternoon because I'm speaking at a leadership class we have for aspiring future officers of the company.' Can I ask someone else to do it? The answer is 'No.'"

Despite the unflinching dedication of leaders like Owens, in these impatient times, leaders come and go, whether they are leaders in politics, business, education, sport, or elsewhere. Short-term pressures, already intense, are intensifying. In the business world, the pressures are especially acute. Trigger-happy investors look for new blood at the slightest suggestion that the pace of growth is slackening.

The result is an acceleration in the turnover of CEOs and a variety of other C-suite executives. I read a business book recently, and virtually all the business leaders quoted had moved on from their jobs. The expectation is that leaders barely stay around long enough to change the pictures on the wall. I became CEO in September 2006. Within two weeks, analysts asked me, "So how long do you want to be in the job? Your predecessors have lasted only two and a half, three years." That's a fair question, but one you'd rather not be asked. I explained that I was 41, I didn't want to be out of a job at age 44, and I'm confident in my ability to get things done.

Even so, a lot of statistics make you question the wisdom of being in a top job. The average tenure of CEOs is now just 18 to 24 months. A study by Murray Steele and Vivien Harrington, two academics from the Cranfield School of Management, revealed that the United Kingdom's top 350 quoted companies change their CEO an average of every five years. CEOs at the top 100 companies fare even worse, with 72 percent in the role for less than five years. (Only 7 percent of CEOs in the top 100 quoted companies have survived over ten years.)

The annual survey of CEO turnover by consulting firm Booz Allen Hamilton makes similarly depressing reading for CEOs. Its 2007 survey revealed that although the CEO's position remains precarious, signs indicate that CEO turnover is reaching a plateau. From 1995 to 2006, annual CEO turnover grew by 59 percent. Globally, however, in 2006, 357 CEOs at the 2,500 largest public companies left office, a 1.2 percent decrease from 2005. Turnover declined in North America, Japan, and the Asia–Pacific region from the 2005 level, with a slight increase in Europe. In 2006, slightly more than one-third of departing CEOs were forced to resign because of either poor performance or disagreements with the board. As a consolation, this isn't limited to

CEOs—the churn of chairmen and chief financial officers (CFOs) is also on the rise. Top jobs should come with a longevity warning.

It's not as if business leaders are especially venerated by people. They increasingly appear to be bracketed with politicians and journalists in unpopularity lists. CEOs are going through a difficult period in terms of public perception. A Bloomberg/*Los Angeles Times* poll in 2007 found that more than 60 percent of people surveyed said CEOs are "not too ethical" or "not ethical at all." Only one-third considered CEOs "mostly ethical." Plus, more than 80 percent believe that CEOs are paid too much.

"There is a public cynicism toward CEO leadership in the air," says Bennis. "The corporate smell from the corporate scandals probably will affect the pool of people who want to do the job of CEO. That may not be obvious at present. But there is a stench in the air, and that could affect the kinds of people who go into corporate leadership worldwide."

All this results in a simmering debate about whether the job of leading a large organization is simply too much. "I don't think the job is impossible—CEOs just need to be more thoughtful," says management expert James Champy. "They need to step back and think about the nature of their business. If they do that, then I think the job is doable. I actually think it's a great time to be a CEO. Sure, there are some irrational demands placed on them, but they need to think their way through that.

Champy also points out that CEOs must walk a fine line between personal ambition and public perception. "When we read about [someone] who has been brought in as CEO, we read about their stock options and the company's current plight. There's very little written about their ambitions. When the CEO tries to explain his or her vision to their people in the company, it tends to be too broad—which makes it weak. It's very seldom personal to them. If you expose your personal ambitions, you are much more likely to engage people than talking about vision. But CEOs are uncomfortable with that. They are fearful of making themselves vulnerable. I believe truly great managers are prepared to make themselves vulnerable. But this means they could be wrong." The trouble is that being wrong can cost you your top job.

Smelling of Roses

The pressure is high, but, after all, most people in top jobs get big bucks for their trouble. Indeed, today's business leaders are rewarded more handsomely than ever. *Forbes* magazine's 2006 survey of executive pay revealed that the average salary for the bosses of America's 500 biggest companies was $10.9 million. That's without perks, stock options, pension, change in control agreements, or deferred compensation. And many leaders who are paid millions of dollars still produce below-average returns for stockholders.

Research by the Associated Press (AP) on executive pay revealed that compensation for America's top CEOs has rocketed in the past few years. The top ten earners were from a range of industries and were all paid at least $30 million each in 2006. Of the 386 companies the AP looked at, only 6 reported that their CEOs earned less than $1 million the previous year.

High salaries are often justified by a shortage of talent. This is true but not as persuasive as it might be. After all, the United States is currently facing a shortage of nurses that the Health Resources and Services Administration predicts will grow to more than one million nurses by 2020. The average salary for a staff nurse is about $47,000, with no stock options.

Finding leaders isn't hard; finding the *right* person for the particular job is. The reality is, people in top jobs are highly paid because leadership comes with a premium price tag.

I've talked about this with Gerry Roche, senior chairman of Heidrick & Struggles. This bare job title doesn't do Roche justice. He has more than 35 years of experience as a recruiter and has worked with hundreds of corporations and their boards. He has identified top executives throughout the world in almost every function and industry, probably placing more people in top jobs than any other recruiter. He joined Heidrick & Struggles back in 1964. Little wonder that one poll nominated Roche as "Recruiter of the Century."

Roche believes that the Renaissance men and women required as the very top leaders are in short supply. But rarity doesn't mean they are extinct. He points to Welch, McNerney, and Bill George of Medtronic as proof that they do exist. "It's just that they are rare breeds; these are the corporate management stars," says Roche. "And they're worth what they make in a supply-and-demand world. There is a lot written suggesting we overpay our business leaders. But think what we pay rock stars and football players. Think of the basketball player Lebron James, who came out of high school and got a $100 million contract from Nike. Now, is that fair? Does that make sense? No. But they said, this guy's going to take the Cleveland Cavaliers to the championship, and he did. So is he worth it? It's supply and demand."

Business leaders aren't sports stars, but they are playing a high-stakes game. We can talk about the rights and wrongs of executive pay all day. But for the people actually doing the job, money is a sideshow. I have yet to meet a leader who is motivated solely by money. Obviously, money is important, but it is nowhere near as important as people might think. The challenge of leading a large organization, or turning round a failing company, or just plain competing and winning, are often more important motivating factors.

I asked Richard Baker what motivated him. His reply was quick: "The challenge of leadership. It is the ultimate personal test, and it can be fantastically rewarding and exciting. You have enormous responsibility. Boots in the U.K. is a huge national institution. You are in charge of a great army. As CEO, it is your decision, but it is also a position of privilege." Any one in a top job or contemplating one must always bear this in mind: Any leadership role in any organization is a privilege.

Key Points

- C-suite (for example, CEO, CFO, CMO, and so on) tenure is shortening. Any would-be leader must bear this reality in mind.
- Before applying for or agreeing to become a leader, you must think of what the job entails, the pressures that come with it, and whether you are ready for it at this stage in your career.

Resources

Bennis, Warren, and James O'Toole. "Don't Hire the Wrong CEO." *Harvard Business Review* (May 2000).

Bloomberg News, "Americans in Poll Hit Ethics, Pay of CEOs." *Boston Globe*, 14 June 2007.

Burson Marsteller. *Building CEO Capital* (2001).

Champy, James, and Nitin Nohria. *The Arc of Ambition* (New York: Perseus, 2001).

Forbes magazine 2006 executive pay report. Available at www.forbes.com/2006/04/17/06ceo_ceo-compensation_land.html.

George, Bill, David Gergen, and David Sims. *True North: Discover Your Authentic Leadership* (San Francisco: Jossey-Bass, 2007).

Ghosn, Carlos, and Philippe Ries. *Shift: Inside Nissan's Historic Revival* (New York: Currency, 2006).

Goffee, Rob, and Gareth Jones. *Why Should Anyone Be Led By You?* (Boston: Harvard Business School Press, 2006).

Gratton, Lynda. *Hot Spots* (San Francisco: Berrett Koehler, 2007).

Hamori, Monika, and Peter Capelli. "The Path to the Top." NBER working paper, May 2004.

Khurana, Rhakesh. "The Curse of the Superstar CEO." *Harvard Business Review* (September 2002).

Knowledge@Wharton. "Want to Win? Here's Some Practical Advice from Jack Welch," 1 June 2005.

Lucier, Chuck, Steven Wheeler, and Rolf Habbel. "CEO Succession 2006: The Era of the Inclusive Leader" (Booz Allen's annual CEO succession study). *Strategy+Business*, Summer 2007.

Steele, Murray. "Challenges of Leadership: The Life and Times of the CEO," Cranfield School of Management Centre for Business Performance, 1999.

The Economist. "Tough at the Top." 23 October 2003.

Useem, Jerry. "Jim McNerney Thinks He Can Turn 3M from a Good Company into a Great One—with a Little Help from His Former Employer, General Electric," *Fortune*, 8 December 2002.

2

Getting There

Every leader is unique. Every journey to the leadership suite is different. But what do you really need to know about the route to the top job?

"The ideal person is someone who has a successful and demonstrable record in doing and planning; someone who has a proven record with experience in running profit centers, staff support functions, and, especially, the strategic planning function within a corporation. Now, if you have somebody that can strategize and execute, and you've got a record that they have done it successfully, then you're home."

—*Gerry Roche, Senior Chairman, Heidrick & Struggles*

My Route

There's no uncomplicated answer to how you should go about building a career that leads to a top job. Hundreds of books have been written about careers. Yet no one I ever meet has a career like the ones you read about. In the books, careers are planned, orderly, linear. One thing leads to another. If you can pull it off, it's quite an achievement, but in my experience, careers are messy, spontaneous, and exciting. Careers are actually the story of your life.

Consider the career of Peter Sharpe, president and CEO of Cadillac Fairview Corporation. "I started out life as a banker, and then I was in sports promotion and public relations for a number of years. In the early 1970s, I was out having a drink with an old buddy of mine from university. I was looking for a new job that would pay over $10,000 a year. And he said, 'Well, we're hiring property managers.' I said, 'What does that pay?' And he said, 'Twelve thousand dollars.' I said, 'Home run! What do they do?' And that's how I got into the business. It's been a business that I've loved. I can honestly say I really look forward to every day. I enjoy seeing the company succeed and mostly enjoy seeing the people succeed."

I am the CEO of the world's top executive search firm (but then, I'm biased). My route to this job doesn't read like a book (although my starting point was a book). I was working in banking in the United States and reading a book that argued that learning Japanese would be crucial to businesses of the future. At the time, this made sense. Japan was the industrial juggernaut. Then I got a call from my old college roommate, who happened to be living in Japan. He told me about a teaching job there and asked me to come over. That was November.

By January, I was out in the middle of the Japanese countryside. Nobody spoke English. Japanese restaurateurs put models of food in their windows, and to order a meal, I had to take the restaurant owners outside and point to what I wanted. Every day I ended up eating noodles, an immediate lesson in the importance of communication and the limitations of noodles as a diet. After ten days, I was tired of noodles and ready to go home.

In time, I made progress, taught at a kindergarten, and continued to study Japanese. In 1992, I moved to Tokyo and realized I wanted to get some work experience in Japan before I went back to the United States. I approached a headhunting company to try to get a job in banking. They offered me a job. I wasn't keen, but I had very little money, so I took the job. My thinking was that I'd work a few months, save some money, and then look elsewhere. But after three months, I was really enjoying the job and the opportunity it gave me to engage with people and help organizations.

Later I returned to New York for a couple years. PA Consulting hired me then to run its Tokyo operation. From there, I joined Heidrick & Struggles, to set up its Financial Services Practice in Japan. At 32 years old, I was very young for such a job, and a number of senior people didn't feel I was experienced enough. (One advantage I have always had is looking older than I actually am.)

While working at Heidrick & Struggles, I earned an MBA from Duke University's Fuqua Business School. I got up at 5:30 each morning to study for a couple hours before work, and then I studied 8–10 hours on the weekend. Thank goodness I had only one child at that time. In September 2002, I became the head of Asia–Pacific for the firm, and in 2005, I combined this role with leading the firm in Europe, the Middle East, and Africa.

Truth be told, I had never dreamed of becoming a CEO. Before I was asked to run Asia–Pacific for Heidrick & Struggles, I just wasn't interested in leadership. I remember saying to the person who was running Asia at the time I was asked to take over, "You could have told me Martians had landed outside and I would have been less surprised than you asking me to take on this role." I was surprised because I simply hadn't thought of it.

When the CEO job came up, I was approached as an internal candidate. As is usually the case, the company also had some external candidates. For any candidate for a top job, even becoming part of the process is a big decision. When you're asked to compete, you have to think about what's right for the business at that time, what's right for you, and what's right for your family. I needed to think along these lines: If they hire someone else, do I leave the firm because I've been here nine years? For the first time, I was thinking about leaving the firm that I loved. This was a major struggle for me, as it is for many people. As an individual, you see the changes you've already made and you know what you would do if you got the CEO role. But are you ready to really put yourself on the line? In the final analysis, the only person who can answer this is you.

In my case, I realized I was still young and could perhaps get a CEO job later. I could have waited a couple years. From a personal view, my family and I loved England, so it was personally a big decision (because I knew it would mean a relocation to the company headquarters in Chicago). I also had a couple other organizations talking to me about doing something else—and I think most CEOs have this just before they are signed up.

I went through the same interviewing process as everyone else. I met every member of the board individually, though I was helped by having attended a few board meetings previously, so I knew each one of them.

This was actually a useful process because it allowed me to be introspective. The board members grilled me about my weaknesses (and told me what they believed my weaknesses were) and asked me how I was going to address them. When you think that very few senior executives get formal career coaching and assessment, at that stage in my career, it was very beneficial. It made me think about myself, the firm, and what I needed to do to grow as a leader and as a person. I still have those thoughts and intentions written down.

The Route Map

But what do you need to do to make the grade, to receive the top-floor office or the keys to the C-suite? The days of the leader who worked his or her way up from the factory floor with no college education appear to be over (if they ever existed).

The latest *Route to the Top* study by Dr. Elisabeth Marx, a partner in Leadership Consulting in the London office of Heidrick & Struggles, highlights the changing career profiles of those leading the FTSE

100 companies and provides an intriguing point of comparison with U.S. executives. Take a look at its main conclusions:

1. Super CEOs are on the rise in the United Kingdom but are not prevalent in the United States.

   Super CEOs (those extremely young CEOs, aged 45 or below) are on the rise in the United Kingdom, with 12 Super CEOs in the FTSE 100, compared to 6 in 1996. In comparison, the Fortune 100 has only two Super CEOs. An earlier analysis of the U.K. Super CEOs showed that these executives structure their careers differently: They are better educated, have worked for a larger number of companies, and stayed shorter periods of time in previous roles, compared to the older age group. In essence, they gain more diverse experience in a shorter period of time. The U.K. Super CEOs are less likely to come from an accountancy/finance background, which is indicative of an overall decline in this type of background in the FTSE 100.

2. Accountancy/finance is in decline in the United Kingdom but on the rise in the United States.

   Finance and accountancy backgrounds are in decline among CEOs in the United Kingdom. In 2002, 41 percent of FTSE 100 CEOs had begun their careers in these sectors; in 2005, this was 38 percent, and in 2007, the figure had fallen to 34 percent.

   Meanwhile, external CEO recruitment is on the rise, with internal CEO promotions at the lowest level in the 11-year history of this study (66 percent). The FTSE 100's internally promoted CEOs are more likely to come from an accountancy/finance early career background (38 percent compared to 21 percent of externally recruited company leaders).

   So the message would seem to be this: If you come from accountancy/finance in the United Kingdom, you're better off staying where you are and working your way up through the ranks. If you have a sales/marketing background, you can expect to move from company to company, as you leapfrog your way to the top. And this career path is likely to include a foreign posting, too: Seventy-six percent of externally recruited CEOs in the United Kingdom have international experience, compared to 63 percent of those who are internally promoted.

The situation in the United States is slightly different: The percentage of CEOs from an early accountancy/finance background is still lower than in the United Kingdom (26 percent, compared to 34 percent), but accountants and financiers are increasingly taking up U.S. CEO positions. Indeed, CEOs under the age of 55 are more likely to come from an accountancy/finance early career background, compared to older CEOs in the index (32 percent versus 20 percent).

3. Founder CEOs are unique to the United States.

Unlike in the FTSE 100, several founders of Fortune 100 companies remain as CEOs. These include Michael Dell at Dell, Frederick Smith at FedEx, Angelo Mozilo at Countrywide Financial, and Jim Sinegal at Costco.

4. Elite education is on the rise.

In both the United Kingdom and the United States, further education is mandatory, and elite education is preferred. Only 4 percent of the FTSE 100 leaders do not hold a university degree (compared to 37.4 percent in 1996). In the United States, 59 percent of Fortune 100 CEOs also have an advanced degree, compared to 45 percent in the United Kingdom. As might be expected, the MBA is one of the most popular degrees, with 32 percent of Fortune 100 CEOs holding this qualification, compared to 16 percent in the FTSE 100.

Thirty-three percent of the Fortune 100 have an Ivy League education; in the United Kingdom, elite university backgrounds are increasing—26 percent of CEOs possess Oxbridge or

Harvard degrees, compared to only 18.7 percent in 1996. This is the highest percentage in 11 years. The FTSE Super CEOs (those under the age of 45) predominantly have an elite education (50 percent compared to 21 percent of the older generation). Similarly, in the Fortune 100, CEOs under the age of 55 are more likely than the older leaders to have a Harvard degree (24 percent compared to 8 percent of older CEOs).

5. Where are the women?

A common feature of the Fortune 100 and the FTSE is also the least impressive: the low number of female CEOs. In the United States, women CEOs number just two. The FTSE has seen a small increase, from no women in 1996 to three today: Marjorie Scardino at Pearson, Cynthia Carroll at Anglo-American, and Dorothy Thompson at Drax. Scardino and Carroll are both American, and all three were externally recruited.

6. Internal promotion is prevalent in the United Kingdom's "most admired companies."

This observation is relevant only to the United Kingdom but provides insight into what makes a good company great. Each year, *Management Today* magazine ranks the United Kingdom's "Most Admired" companies. Looking at this, the companies that appear in the FTSE 100 have significantly more internally promoted CEOs (86 percent) than externally recruited leaders. This balks the U.K. trend and suggests strong succession management in these organizations.

Other interesting research in this area comes from Monika Hamori at the Instituto de Empresa Business School in Madrid. In a major study, she analyzed the resumes of the CEOs of the 500 largest companies in both the United States and Europe (1,000 in all). Hamori's study suggests that career paths have changed in the past decade in four important ways. First, the loyal company man or woman is increasingly rare. The second career shift is that executives are evaluated against much higher, more rigorous performance standards. Booz Allen Hamilton's annual CEO study shows that the percentage of CEOs dismissed for performance-based reasons has quadrupled since the mid-1990s.

The third change is a move toward younger appointments based on merit. "Today's corporate landscape presents greater opportunities for those who want to reach the top of corporate hierarchies," says Hamori. "My research with Professor Peter Cappelli at Wharton [School, University of Pennsylvania] shows that high performers are appointed to CEO and executive positions about four years younger than they were 20 years ago."

The final change, she says, is that single-industry and single-job-function careers are declining. "Executives who have worked in multiple industries and multiple job functions—and, therefore, have an eclectic management experience—are much more appreciated and in demand today than a couple years ago," she says. "Single-function executives represent a tiny minority these days, and their proportion keeps decreasing."

Career Logistics

So I've told you how I came to a top job. I'm not saying that's the way you should do it. And I don't want to sound glib. The point is that I didn't really think and believe I would be a CEO until the phone call came through confirming it. And I remember that phone call well. I was sitting in my office in London when the phone rang. I picked it up, and there was a female voice saying, "Could you hold for Dick Beattie, please?" (Beattie is the chairman of Simpson Thacher & Bartlett LPP and the lead director of Heidrick & Struggles.) I knew what this was about! The ten seconds it took to connect us were the longest of my life; time seemed to come to a total halt. And then there was Beattie, saying, "Kevin, we would like to offer you the job of CEO." Only then did I believe I could ever be a CEO. I saw Beattie in an elevator a few weeks after the call, and he laughed as he remembered that conversation. "I really got you that day, didn't I?" Yes, he certainly did.

The route to the top is virtually always a long and somewhat winding road. One successful executive told me that the failure of his first marriage was a key point in his learning and development. He had previously been filled with the blind confidence of the successful. He thought that he could communicate with anyone. The breakdown of his marriage taught him otherwise. He then found himself running a house and a business. "I think it helped make me more empathetic with people," he admitted. "Without that experience, quite frankly, I would've not been at all empathetic. There were some tough lessons but some character-building things that helped me be a better leader and helped me relate to other people."

Carlos Ghosn, president and CEO of auto manufacturer Nissan, and president and CEO of Renault, is the benchmark for the truly global, successful business leader. He is Brazilian-born but was brought up in Lebanon and educated in France. His career has been equally mobile. He worked with Michelin for 18 years. First, he was a plant manager in Le Puy, France; then head of research and development for industrial tires in Ladoux, France; and then the chief operating officer of Michelin's South American activities based in Brazil. From there, he became the chairman and CEO of Michelin North America. There he restructured the company after it acquired the Uniroyal Goodrich Tire Company in 1990.

Ghosn went on in 1996 to become the executive vice president of the Renault Group. In addition to supervising Renault activities in the Mercosur, he was responsible for advanced research, car engineering and development, car manufacturing, power train operations, and purchasing. He joined Nissan as its chief operating officer in June 1999, became its president in June 2000, and was named CEO in June 2001. At the time he joined, Nissan was $20 billion in debt and only 3 of its 48 models were generating a profit. Ghosn claimed that Nissan would have no net debt by 2005. One year after he arrived, Nissan's net profit climbed to $2.7 billion from a loss of $6.1 billion in the previous year. He also became president of Renault in May 2005.

Ghosn's route to the top is a classic experience-based one. Over the past 30 years, he has worked and led throughout the world in a variety of roles and functions. This is a pattern that emerges repeatedly among leaders. No matter which sector they come from, most have clocked a lot of experience in a lot of different businesses and business functions.

Consider Gary Knell, the CEO of Sesame Workshop, the not-for-profit educational organization behind *Sesame Street*. His business is about a million miles distant from Ghosn's world in the automotive industry, but in talking to Gary, their issues are often similar. "In a non-profit, there is what I would call a double bottom line: a quantitative set of measures which are probably consistent with the for-profit world and then an expectation that you're making an impact on society. If you're not making that impact, you're not going to get the income you need to survive," Knell explains.

In addition, Knell's route to the top bore some remarkable similarity to Ghosn's. Knell began with a background in journalism and law and politics. He began working in Washington, D.C., in the late 1970s as staff counsel on the U.S. Senate Judiciary Committee. He proceeded to work in public broadcasting and got to really know the television business at WNET/Channel 13 in New York. Then he jumped over to Sesame Workshop, in the business affairs and legal unit, and was promoted to chief administrative officer. Knell says this helped him understand the backbone of the organization and learn everything from information systems to marketing, to human resources, to the senior executive team. "In some ways, there was a natural progression in my career," Knell says. "It gave me the experience to know what makes the corporation run and the importance of managing people. That led to a progression and some global experience and then finally becoming CEO."

Career Evolution

Monika Ribar is the president and CEO of Panalpina, a global transport and logistics company that employs 14,000 people and operates a network of about 500 offices with branches in 90 countries. She is particularly interesting because she came up through a succession of top jobs in the company. Ribar took over as CEO in 2006 at the age of 47 after being the company's CIO (chief information officer) and then CFO. Her accumulated experiences in top jobs helped make her a natural candidate. But she points out that this was more a process of evolution than a plan.

"Over the last five or six years, I have said that if I got the opportunity, I would like to manage a company and to have the full responsibility of being CEO," she says. "It was not something I was totally fixed on—but I think I have learned a lot and I have seen a lot, and I think I could do the job in a slightly different way."

But even after 16 years with the company and a huge variety of experience, Ribar believes that the CEO job is unique. "The CFO job in a company is a very, very important job, but still you are sharing responsibility. As the CEO, it's you—period."

This certainly struck a chord with my own experience. As you grow up in a firm, you encounter a lot of different individuals, but they tend to look at only their pieces of the puzzle, whether it's finance, operations, or technology. As the CEO, you have to look at the whole organization. And you quickly realize that if you pull one lever, it affects everything else.

Ribar believes that her background in financial control encouraged her to look at the company in broader terms. Her range of experience within the company was also helpful. "I did different jobs: I did a lot of projects, including IT, which is very important for a logistics company. And now, being the CEO, one of the main things is to put the right people in the right positions because you can't do it yourself anymore," she says. "Take IT: I don't have a technical background at all, and there were people who were probably not that happy when I took over as CIO, but I managed and nobody left. The people who were not happy are still here, and they were very unhappy when I left IT. So I think I have learned to deal with people and to motivate them whatever their likes and dislikes.'

Get on with the Job

Before Jim Skinner became CEO of McDonald's, he was the president of the organization and worked closely with Jack Greenberg. He became the vice chairman during Jim Cantalupo's regime and then worked as Charlie Bell's right-hand man. Skinner says that gave him the opportunity to pick and choose things. "The interesting thing for me was that I had the opportunity to observe the behavior of my predecessors at very close hand," he says. "At McDonald's, people would say, 'When did you know you could do the job?' I would say, 'Well, I always felt I could do the job, but you know you're ready to do the job when you're critical of the performance of the individual who's doing the job. You're able to say, 'Well, I wouldn't have done it that way.' Now, you're not critical about it publicly, but in your own mind, you sort of sense, 'Wait a minute, I could probably do that job.'"

A time comes when a top job is within your reach. In talking to leaders, I have found that the top job suddenly becomes clear and achievable, like a summit above the clouds. The leaders I have met are ambitious, but they have not made their ambition the cornerstone of their being and their work.

Consider Richard Baker, former CEO of Alliance Boots. After Baker took over as CEO, he led Boots to a successful merger with Alliance UniChem. "I was never hung up on the title of CEO," he told me. "From an early age, I organized things, whether it was at Cub Scouts or on the sports field. I was organizing, communicating, and leading. It was a logical conclusion to become a CEO. I enjoy leading."

Driven and ambitious, some are natural leaders, but all would-be leaders ensure that they deliver on the job at hand. Roche sums this up in characteristically robust fashion: "The best way to get your next job is to do a good job at the job you're in, and not be distracted by positioning and posturing yourself for the next role. The minute you start distracting yourself from your current responsibilities to choreograph your next job, the trouble can start. We see all the time people who come to us and say, 'I have a good job where I am a COO [chief operating officer], but I want to be a CEO—can you help me do that?' And they do that with us and with all our competitors. We wind up thinking that he's spending more time on where he's going than succeeding where he is."

Roche champions a different approach: "My thinking is that the best way to get a promotion or get a new job is to excel at what you're doing. Trust me, we will find you. Your managers will wind up saying, 'Hey, there's a guy down there who's knocking the ball out of the park like crazy—let's put him into finance for a while and round him out so that when we're looking for our next president, he's a candidate.' That's the way it usually happens and should happen. You can't allow yourself to get distracted with politicking, choreographing, and stylizing for the future at the expense of short-changing the job for which you are responsible. At the same time, you need to do some strategic planning of your own and say, 'Hey, if I'm ever going to get to run GE, I'd better go get a tour in finance and in strategic planning—running a profit center alone won't do it.'"

In terms of managing my own career, I measured it by my performance. I did what was asked of me to the very best of my abilities, for my bosses and for my clients. I just got on with the job at hand and didn't spend all my time looking at the horizon.

In the Ascendancy

As Roche suggests, the normal journey to top management is to rise up through operations, not necessarily through staff positions. Future leaders generally have experience running profit centers. Think of Ghosn's or Skinner's career progression. At GE, all those in the frame to succeed Jack Welch—Jeff Immelt, Jim McNerney, Bob Nardelli, (now CEO of Chrysler) and so on—had run large profit centers.

Some rise via the job of COO. "The single most dominant functional background for a chief operating officer is running things, execution," says Roche. "When you're picking a COO, the questions are: does this person know the elements of getting a job done, can he execute that job, can he do things, can he see that things are done, can he produce the bottom line? Those are the talents of a COO."

Having a CEO with the ability to run different profit centers is a good idea, but there's no cookie-cutter template for the CEO—or any other top job. Steve Tappin leads Heidrick & Struggles' CEO and board practice in the United Kingdom. To keep up-to-date with the marketplace, during 2007, he interviewed the CEOs of 67 of the FTSE 100. Tappin's conclusions are intriguing and varied. "I think what was surprising was just the diversity of the different types of CEOs," he told me. Some CEOs are very entrepreneurial—in the U.K., he points to Charlie Dunstone at Carphone Warehouse and Martin Sorrell at WPP. Others, such as Allan Leighton (the former CEO of retailer Asda, who brought in to help the loss-making Royal Mail), excel in turnarounds and operational performance improvement. Yet another group are international consolidators, such as John Browne during his time at BP. Still others are business transformers who refocus the business and transform it. "Some CEOs are better in certain types of situations," Tappin says.

In his research, Tappin differentiates between the CEOs who can be termed "professional managers" and those who are, first and foremost, leaders. "*Professional managers* could be seen as a negative term, but what I mean by that is that they're generalists," he explains. "They're pretty good at strategy, pretty good with people, pretty good at execution; they build a good team around them, and they succeed in that way. And there's also a group of CEOs who are very strong leaders. Some of the best CEOs have the appetite to lead from the front when they need to and make some of the important calls for the business, but they are equally comfortable in developing other leaders—empowering them, training them in the culture for them to actually lead within a business. There's a small group of people who can do that. For a lot of them, the root of their success lies in some of their personal qualities."

Similarly, Roche's starting point for all his work is that every single executive is different: "I have a line that I like a lot. Oliver Wendell Holmes said, 'No generality is worth a damn, including this one.' Well, I know a lot of CEOs, and no two of them are alike."

The message is clear: *Vive la différence!* In their book *Why Should Anyone Be Led By You?*, Rob Goffee and Gareth Jones have distilled this down to this simple advice: "Be yourself—more—with skill."

The Glass Ceiling Remains

The continuing absence of women from the top jobs in the business world is important to mention at this stage. The Lehman Brothers Centre for Women in Business at London Business School surveyed 61 European companies and other organizations to determine how they measure and manage gender issues. Amazingly, women hold only 15 percent of senior executive positions in Europe. (The encouraging news in Europe is that 50 to 60 percent of graduate recruits joining European businesses are now women, although it is still anticipated that women will occupy only 20 percent of senior roles by 2017.) The results are similarly disappointing and unrepresentative no matter where you look in the world. The glorious exception is Norway, where, thanks to legislation, 40 percent of board members are now women. The last time I looked at the stats, around 13 percent of Fortune 500 board members were women.

Lynda Gratton, professor of management practice at London Business School, explains the reasons for the continuing paucity of women at the top of organizations. "There is a clear gap between policy rhetoric and practical reality," she says. "Policies such as flexible working and part-time working can be crucial to women as they move up the corporate ladder. Yet while most companies have these policies, few actually use them. Less than 10 percent of female managers actually adopt flexible working, and less than 20 percent of managers and senior executives work part-time."

Gratton points to the need to change the corporate environment to better suit women's needs. "The challenge here is not creating the policy, but rather establishing an environment in which it is seen to be legitimate to take these options," she says. "Creating a place where both men and women feel able to work flexibly would do much to reduce the leaky pipeline of female talent and, indeed, create more humane places of work for men." Gratton also laments the lack of women at the world's business schools, which she estimates at about 20 percent.

Little wonder that the women at the top of organizations are usually remarkable and that their experiences are very different from those of their male colleagues. Ribar admits that being a lone woman in a room full of men is hardly a new experience for her. At her business school, women accounted for a mere 14 percent of students. Gender differences also have a direct impact in terms of social norms: "You need to know people, and this is probably easier for a man than a woman. If a colleague CEO asks me for lunch or for dinner, it's a different story if you do that as a man and a woman or if you do that as two men or two women. Something which, in the man's community, is totally normal, all of a sudden gets viewed differently. Our society has to get used to this and be able to deal with it as normal."

Learning...Always

The key to developing as a potential and actual leader is a willingness to learn as you go along. I learned a great deal in my first Asia–Pacific leadership role about restructuring, letting people go, rebuilding, entering new markets, and handling personalities. That's when I began to learn about change and how people handle it. If you want to change the firm and the organization, sometimes you have to take people out, and that never gets any easier. I also learned the importance of providing coaching and feedback to individuals. You need to be direct from the beginning. I used to try to work with people and say, "Look, could you think about doing this?" or "Would you mind doing that?" and they wouldn't get the message. I learned that, as uncomfortable as it is, you must be direct and clear. Leaders have too many demands on their time to keep going back to the same conversations. Being direct isn't easy. I used to find it uncomfortable, particularly when giving people bad news, but I've learned that this is the best way to handle your time, to handle change, and to get things done.

Key Points

- No one-size-fits-all instant career guide can help you become a leader. Every career and every leader is different.
- Most successful leaders learn as they go along. They work hard at learning always. They are also skilled at execution but, critically, they combine this with knowledge of planning and strategy.

Resources

George, Bill, David Gergen, and David Sims. *True North: Discover Your Authentic Leadership* (San Francisco: Jossey-Bass, 2007).

Ghosn, Carlos, and Philippe Ries. *Shift: Inside Nissan's Historic Revival* (New York: Currency, 2006).

Goffee, Rob, and Gareth Jones. *Why Should Anyone Be Led By You?* (Boston: Harvard Business School Press, 2006).

Gratton, Lynda. *Hot Spots* (San Francisco: Berrett Koehler, 2007).

Hamori, Monika, and Peter Capelli. "The Path to the Top." NBER working paper, May 2004.

Marx, Elisabeth. *Route to the Top*. (London: Heidrick & Struggles, 2007).

3

My First 100 Days

One hundred days is only a short time, and far shorter when everyone inside the company and out is watching your every move. So what does the new leader need to do before taking the job and when the first day beckons?

"I used almost all of the first 100 days to talk to people in operations. I went to the company's battlefields rather than staying at head office and getting reports from a lot of managers. I went and talked to the soldiers."

—Takeshi Niinami, CEO, Lawson

What Are You Walking Into?

Starting a new job is never easy. You encounter new people, a new office, and new expectations. For anyone entering a top job, these issues are magnified. Whether you're coming in to head a division, run a department, take over a region, or manage the entire outfit, people are watching and waiting. It's similar to being in a goldfish bowl— perhaps that's why so many executive offices have fish tanks.

Today's CEOs have a tougher job than their predecessors but not necessarily because of their corporate responsibilities. "I don't think the leaders are expected to do anything more today," reflects McDonald's CEO Jim Skinner. "I think they probably delivered as much in the past as they have today, but the scrutiny is greater. From performance to governance, to pay, to lifestyle, the job is a more public job today than it has been in the past. The scrutiny is simply greater." Everyone is watching—sometimes literally.

The reality of a top job can be daunting. The money might be good, but job security is low and diminishing, and the job itself rarely presents a clean and happy start. Takeshi Niinami, CEO of convenience-store chain Lawson (30 percent owned by Mitsubishi), recalls his early days with mixed emotions. "I think during the first 100 days, I was a very severe leader. I made cuts and, from the employees' point of view, I was a bad leader. I'd come from a big company, Mitsubishi, and nobody knew who I was. The first 100 days were really a mistake in terms of morale and motivating people—I couldn't motivate people at all."

Takeshi's honesty is brutal, but the situation he inherited was bad and worsening. "The company was not doing very well. When I arrived, profits were on their way to sinking from $405 million to $340 million. But there was no feeling of crisis among people. They thought, 'We're still making profits, what's wrong?' It was very hard to create a feeling that there was a crisis among the rank and file."

The challenging truth countless new hires have experienced is that if a company needs you, a problem often—not always—exists. Of course, you know that problems exist. Every company in the world has problems; your company wouldn't have recruited a new division head if everything was fine in the division. But rest assured, the problems are always worse than you think. New leaders regularly walk into unpredictable and unstable situations. Morale might be low. Employees—and shareholders—might be confused about the organization's direction. Performance is likely down. Enter a new leader—often into a new organization, frequently into a new industry.

Rose on Retail

One of the best examples I have encountered is the story of Stuart Rose. After working for the U.K. retailer Marks & Spencer (M&S), Rose worked for the Burton Group, Argos, Booker, and Arcadia. As his career had taken off, M&S's fortunes had declined. In May 2004, M&S's chairman, Luc Vandevelde, announced his departure. Soon afterward, Rose had a Thursday morning meeting with nonexecutive director Kevin Lomax. A few hours later, retailer Sir Philip Green launched a hostile takeover for M&S for £8 billion. Later that evening, M&S approached Rose. By the following Monday, Rose was installed as the company's CEO. Being in the right place at the right time is as important at the top of the corporate tree as it is anywhere else.

But before new leaders celebrate their luck, they need to remember that if everything were perfect, they wouldn't need a new leader. No matter what the job, the new hire usually encounters trouble. When Rose took over as CEO, the once-legendary U.K. retailer was on its knees. To put its problems in perspective, M&S was the second-largest market-capitalized retailer in the world after Wal-Mart in 1997; M&S was capitalized at $25 billion and Wal-Mart at $60 billion. By 2005–2006, M&S was capitalized as the twenty-eighth largest retailer, still at $25 billion (having been down to $12 billion), and Wal-Mart was at $300 billion. M&S was saddled with a mountain of £3 billion in inventory. Its clothing range was confusingly branded with 16 subbrands. M&S was slow to move with fashion, and its clothes looked increasingly dowdy in its cluttered high-street stores. Among other problems, consultants were running 31 "strategic projects."

The good news in such circumstances is that the leader might have nothing to lose. "Believe it or not, I don't think they saw me as a white knight; I think they saw me as absolute desperation: 'Well we are not sure he can do it, but he is the last resort, so let's give it a try,'" says Rose. "Obviously, if you come into a business that is in a crisis, you have the disadvantage that you're coming in at a crisis, but actually you have a bigger advantage—the advantage is that the board, frankly, would have agreed to anything. I had absolute control, which was key."

The second advantage Rose had, in both this situation and others before him, was the company's lack of direction. "I've been in a few businesses that have been in a bit of trouble in the last ten years or so, and I think what I spotted fairly early on is that it wasn't as if they were spiraling away in the wrong direction—they just weren't doing anything at all."

Rose spent the first months of his leadership of M&S fighting off Philip Green's unwelcome takeover bid. Not until July 2004 was the specter of a takeover averted. Having a clear, short-term challenge helped focus energies.

The great thing about a crisis is that action is necessary immediately. You don't have time to hatch a complex strategy and then roll it out through the organization. The organization needs someone who can roll up his sleeves and execute. It wasn't so much that the company was continuing to make the wrong decisions; it had made them and was standing amid the results without knowing what to do next.

This situation was made for Rose. "It's a bit like the old stories—people are so desperate for leadership that even if you lead them the wrong way, they'd rather go that way than go nowhere at all. People were almost literally standing around saying either, 'There isn't a problem—what problem?' or 'There is a problem, but we don't know what to do about it.' Some were saying to go left, and some were saying to go right—and the rest, well, it just passed over their heads."

In such a pressured environment, "almost perfect right now" is often better than "complete perfection tomorrow." In a complex and difficult business situation with the press and expectant employees hanging on your every word, the chances of hatching a watertight, perfect strategy are extremely slim. You need to compromise on perfection to execute in accordance with what the company desperately needs. Rose remembers what he told himself: "Be 95 percent right rather than 100 percent right. Follow your gut instincts. Cut back minimally on research; use the benefit of 30 years' experience. You aren't going to be right in every respect, but mostly you could get it right by touch or feel—and then if you are in any doubt at all about doing something today or doing something tomorrow, do it today." Of course, as Rose candidly admits, mistakes are made.

Counting the Days

Not every new hire wrestles with an aggressive takeover bid—but it can feel that way. And then you have the final pressure point: Everyone expects you to put your mark on your job and your team within 100 days.

I asked Skinner about his feelings on the day he took over at McDonald's. His predecessor, Charlie Bell, had to leave the job because of ill health; he had only recently taken over after the tragically young death of previous CEO Jim Cantalupo. "The reaction that I had about the job at McDonald's was really an enormous sense of responsibility and accountability to the organization and the stakeholders in the organization, not the shareholders," says Skinner.

Many people comment on the first 100 days of a leader's tenure. Indeed, the time you have to make an impact is decreasing. "Boards are more willing to toss people out and are giving CEOs a much shorter leash—many senior executives feel they have a much shorter time frame to prove themselves," says former Harvard Business School and INSEAD professor Michael Watkins, author of *The First 90 Days*. (Note the book title—that's another ten days gone.)

Although leaders have less time to make an impression, no defined deadline exists. Leadership is no longer neatly linear—if it ever was. Your first period in charge is a roller coaster. Before boarding a roller coaster, it helps to know what you're getting into. If you understand the process, you're likely to cope with its ups and downs far more effectively.

Tone Setting

Seung-Yu Kim became CEO of the Hana Financial Group in Korea in 1997. The timing was not auspicious. "Our economy was really in trouble," he says. "Our currency was overvalued, and in my first 100 days, 12 of the 30 biggest Korean conglomerates were bankrupted. The last one was Kia Motors, which we had a big exposure to. It went bankrupt on July 20, 1997. I still remember the date."

Kim had been with Hana since the time it had a mere 20 people. Hana developed its commercial banking in the early 1990s, and he was well placed because he had prior experience and a network in commercial banking. However, this did not prepare him for taking over a company at the height of a far-reaching economic crisis. Faced with a crisis, Kim focused on "awakening [his] people," reshaping, and restructuring.

From the start, Kim worked at making all employees feel appreciated. After taking over as CEO in February, he led the purchase of a training center in April. "At the time, we had less than 1,000 people, so every week, in the evening, I met with some of them. In my first 100 days, in particular, I tried to appreciate them one by one."

Surrounded by crisis, Kim increased salaries by a mere 2 percent in 1997, put his own pay increase on hold, and cut costs. "For example, I took economy class when I had a business trip overseas. Most CEOs travel first class, but this was part of me showing my people how much I appreciated and valued them," Kim says. "My people followed me and trusted me, and that's why we overcame the financial crisis." When he insisted on flying economy, the airlines, aware of why he was flying economy, left the neighboring seat vacant.

Kim was in the habit of heading home at nine or ten o'clock at night. On his way home, if he saw any of the bank's branches with their lights on, he stopped off and paid a visit. People working extra hours were regularly treated to pizzas courtesy of the CEO. The pizzas came with a message.

"Whenever I made a surprise visit to our branches, I highlighted the significance of our customers," Kim says. "I always tried to tell people that our shareholders could leave us at any time were we not profitable, but our customers would stay with us if we did our best for them. I also reminded them that they didn't need to look for market trends, as market demand is nothing but the products and services which customers want us to provide them. They listened to me. And now the strong customer/market-oriented philosophy of the early days of Hana Bank has become the core value of the entire group."

As Kim's experience powerfully illustrates, you not only have to hit the ground running at any top job, you must also hit the ground communicating and connecting with people. That might take a lot of pizzas.

My First 100

My own plan for the first 100 days was to figure out who the right people were and to establish whether I had enough of the right people to get us where we needed to go. I had a very clear idea about the direction of the firm and where I wanted to go. The unknown piece at the beginning, even as an insider, is the people. I think most leaders would agree that, in these early days, you find that 20 percent of individuals want to embrace change and get there, 60 percent can go either way, and 20 percent probably have to go because they don't want to change and will do anything they can to throw roadblocks up.

At the same time I was looking internally, I was very keen to re main outward facing. I wanted to keep up my client work because I felt that our firm was too inward-facing. But even though you endeavor to do that, you realize that the internal part of the job needs a lot more attention. It's similar to the game whack-a-mole: Every time you sort out one thing, something else pops up. I don't think that ever stops. Events always dictate the pace.

A great story is told about British Prime Minister Harold Macmillan. He was asked what made the job of prime minister difficult. "Events, dear boy, events," he replied. Every leader knows the feeling.

I remember my first week. I had a great opening 24, even 36, hours, with people calling and congratulating and expressing how hopeful they were. I got calls from the people in Asia whom I had grown up with and the people in Europe, the Middle East, and Africa (EMEA) I had been working with. The Americans were a little more unsure of me, an American out of America. Although I sound American—I *am* an American—my fellow countrymen tend to doubt I'm one of them any longer because I've spent 12 years away. Many people view me as stateless instead of an American. As a leader, it's important be aware of how you're perceived and thought of right from the start. How can you reassure people? Should you reassure them, or is it better to be slightly distant?

Similar to most leaders, I put more pressure on myself than anyone else does—particularly in those first 100 days, you know people are giving you their time and trust, but they want action, and you need to deliver. Every time a new leader comes in, people hope that he or she will change things for the better, but the leader needs to understand that people don't particularly want the change to affect them personally. People want change and action, but they don't want to deal with it directly.

Looking back now, after 18 months (and counting), I don't think I'd do anything differently in terms of those first 100 days. Maybe I would have put less pressure on myself in those first months—because the pressure never lets up, and you just need to keep figuring out what's going on, put your head down, and get things done.

The Art of Preparation

The more I talked to other leaders, the more it became clear that how you start is critical. Consider Richard Baker, who was 40 when he took over as CEO of Boots, which later became Alliance Boots. Baker had worked at Mars, where he was sales director, and Asda before-hand. He was highly experienced and had been the COO at Asda. Even so, he admits that he was "not at all prepared" for the rigors of being a CEO.

"Even as a COO, you tend to stick to a few disciplines. You're at the heart of the action, but you don't need to know how a financial audit works, for example. I'd worked on brands, products, and operations, but I knew little of IT, finance, HR, and so on," Baker admitted. "It was a big leap, and that's why it is the ultimate test. You come up through organizations and develop a particular competence, and then you find yourself running the show. That's the same for most CEOs."

In a business such as Alliance Boots, Baker had to deal with a whole range of technical support functions that are fundamental to the business. As CEO, he soon found himself approving huge invest-ments in IT with limited knowledge of the technical detail.

Because you are suddenly thrust into such alien territory as a new leader, how do you cope? "You need good general-management skills and judgment, and people you can trust, with the technical compe-tence required by the business," says Baker. "The big word is *trust*. You've got to get a team of people together you can trust."

Before taking over at Alliance Boots, Baker had a four-month break to contemplate the job ahead. This is not an unusual situation. I was interested in how he spent this time. It must be a curious period, I thought. Similar to the president-elect, the leader-in-waiting is in limbo, watching and hoping, with limited opportunities to learn more or get involved. Baker spent his time talking to people whose judg-ment he trusted. He talked to suppliers whom he already knew and visited the company's shops to have a look around. He talked to other leaders and took as much advice as possible. He learned about the business from the outside in.

The result was that when he started his new job, Baker had a plan for the first two or three weeks. "In the first two weeks, I interviewed all of the top 30 people at the company," he recalls. "I had a formal questionnaire so they were all asked the same questions. I wanted to find out what they thought worked well and what they would do in my position. They were simple, open questions, and from that I got a good consensus on what we needed to do. Perhaps 25 out of the 30 were saying much the same thing."

Baker was primarily able to keep to his plan in the first few weeks. No sudden crises materialized. He then organized a detailed review of the company's top management team by a recruitment expert. Managers were, in effect, interviewed for their own jobs. Based on this work and Baker's judgments, he made changes to the management team within the first six weeks.

"The first 100 days really are critical—you set the tone," says Baker. "At the first meetings, you can almost see people's antennae twitching. People are looking to see whether you're relaxed, impatient, and so on. First impressions are critical. If you think about it, you do most things once in 100 days."

Flash points might emerge in the unlikeliest of places—at Boots, Baker arrived wearing a shirt and tie, as he had always done in his previous companies, but the dress culture at Boots was more informal. He was asked for his opinion on the dress code. His four months of preparation hadn't covered this issue. "I hadn't planned it but said I thought people weren't dressed professionally enough. We were in a war and I expected people to be dressed for battle. Eventually, I had to sit some of the people down and tell them that was a rule. It was a diktat. That sort of thing sets the tone."

45

The Same but Different

Part of the new job is actively not doing your old job—a particular problem if you have been promoted from within. "The toughest thing to do is to let go of what you used to do—there's a natural inclination when the phone rings to pick it up," says Peter Sharpe, chairman and CEO of Toronto-based Cadillac Fairview Corporation, which co-owns and manages about 80 properties in Canada and the United States, including 15 U.S. shopping centers located primarily on the West Coast. "It's about having the discipline to refer that [to someone else instead of] just dealing with it quickly yourself. It's a real temptation."

Gary Knell, CEO of Sesame Workshop, agreed that the first days are critical. "All of a sudden everyone's looking at you," Knell told me. "It is somewhat lonely, at least certainly in the beginning. All of a sudden you've got to make some judgments and trust that you are getting advice from the variety of quarters that you need. The key is having people whom you trust around you who are going to tell you objectively what's happening."

Listening is key at all times, but even more so when taking on a new leadership role. "The importance of a listening tour shouldn't be underestimated," Knell says. "Even though I was an insider...when you're sitting at the top, people aren't going to open [up] to you in the way that they want to open up to you as a peer. I think it's important that you are spending some time to really learn, from that top position, what are the critical issues and where are the risks and opportunities. After three months or so, you can really apply some change and make some decisions.

Knell also points out that plenty gets thrown at new leaders in those first 100 days. "You've got to actually get right into the thick of the stuff and start making some decisions," he says.

Part of that is to prove yourself to the company. "People test you; they want to test what you're made of—is this going to be somebody who is going to make decisions quickly, take a lot of time, or procrastinate? They want to test your style," says Knell. "People who were formerly your peers are going to look at you in a much different way. Maybe some of them were rivals for the job and have some sort of hurt feelings about it. So it's finding a way to raise people's vision and trying to bring some closure on the process of selection and say, 'Okay, that's been done, we've got to focus now on the future of the company.' You want to inspire people to be part of that solution."

Monika Ribar's situation was somewhat unusual because the company announced that she was to become CEO of Panalpina in June 2006, and she actually began the job in October. This posed a slightly different challenge because she had 100 days before the first 100 days actually began.

"Whatever I did after June was, to some extent, looked at as if I was doing it as the CEO," she says. "It changes from the day you are announced. People react differently; they look at you differently. I don't think that I have changed, but it's the job. When it came to October 1, I don't think that I did anything differently. Of course, I didn't take care of the CFO stuff because I had found my CFO. For me, it was very important that I started to think about how to organize myself. People were always asking me, 'Will you work more now?' And I said, 'No, I can't work more, but I have to work differently.' This is certainly something which I gave a lot of thought to. How do I organize myself? What is my agenda?"

Having clarified her modus operandi and her expectations, Ribar brought together her management team three months into her time in charge. "It took one strategy meeting, which was very hard for me because I needed to align them on the same targets. Then they realized that I'm not against them, that I can help them, that I'm not coming in and changing everything, that I'm interested and want to learn, and that I don't come in and say, 'You know what? I know it better than you do.'"

Understand the Process

These lessons apply to anyone entering a top job. Issues are slightly heightened for the CEO, but they are the same if you are coming in to run a department. People suddenly look to you for leadership. For a leader to emerge unscathed at the end of the first 100 days, it takes focus, energy, and luck. I've found that it takes awhile to move from defense to offense.

As Ribar makes clear, leaders always need to make tough decisions. However, if you are to survive and, eventually, thrive, you must first understand the process that you will experience. Many of the books about leadership focus on personality characteristics. Clearly, these are important, but leaders also must understand the process of leadership—the time lines that will affect them and the likely highs and lows. These are particularly acute during the first few days, weeks, and months in a new leadership role.

The process has four phases: anticipation, exploration, building, and contributing.

Anticipation

Even before starting work, leaders should develop an entry strategy, as Baker showed so clearly. They must look at their role, set expectations, discuss any issues that need immediate clarity, and enter into an honest exchange of views and hopes. Clearly, they need to be careful not to overplay their hand or to become too involved too soon. But you can set the tone even before you enter the building.

Exploration

The time lines are fairly consistent. A honeymoon period exists during the first 90 days of a new leader's tenure—although honeymoons, similar to job tenure, are shortening dramatically. Throughout this time, leaders get to know the organization, the people, and the management team. This is the exploration phase. At this point, the board offers long-term support and promises whatever resources are required.

Even so, the first period is one of intense pressure, which I experienced. Support might come from elsewhere, but leaders tend to initially put pressure on themselves. They have a new job and a new challenge, and they feel a responsibility to deliver. If you really want to be in a top job, that personal pressure can be incredibly intense. After all, you might have spent the last 30 years acquiring the skills and experience to take on a particular job. You have a lot of sweat invested in the job. You desperately want to make it work. And—leaders are only human—you are fearful of failure. You can't bear the thought of screwing it up—all that time and energy and all those dreams disappearing into well-publicized smoke.

Leaders are right to feel pressured. Research suggests that you can trace the roots of failure to what happens within the first 15 days. Common causes include trying to do too much too soon, failing to assimilate the culture, failing to adapt leadership and management styles, and doing insufficient analysis and planning. I come from a generation that didn't grow up with multitasking. We used to joke about not being able to walk down the street and chew gum at the same time. Now you've got your BlackBerry, tickers on the computer screen, earphones, and ringing phones. I grew up in a generation of black-and-white TVs; now everything is in high-definition touch-screen Technicolor. This only cranks up the pressure.

None of this makes life easy for you in your new role. The challenge is that although leaders are often hired to achieve change, resistance always occurs when change actually happens. Leaders can find themselves firmly wedged between the proverbial rock and a hard place. Failure is clearly bad for the individual and expensive for the company—the cost of a failed hire is estimated to be at least four times salary and bonus.

Building

Then the pressure balance changes. The building stage—3 to 14 months—marks a shift in emphasis. The leader has assembled a team, and the onus is on the team to deliver. This is a time when the leader can encounter emotional lows. After the initial rush of excitement, it is easy to feel physically and mentally exhausted. Difficult decisions still need to be made. The leader might need to act on people who are clearly in the wrong roles or are simply unqualified for the tasks required.

"A lot of leaders start off and get some initial momentum. They launch a lot of initiatives and make some changes, like disposing of things or changing the people at the top. And they get into that in the first six months. But I think there's a period after that when they either get a grip of the company and start to lead it, or are just constantly fire-fighting and eventually fail in the role," says Tappin. "I think there's a six- to nine-month window with investors and within the company when you can make some initial changes that are relatively straightforward. But I think the challenge is the next period."

Contributing

The final stage is the contributing stage—beyond 14 months. The leader needs to begin delivering results. Pressure mounts again—this time from the board. No excuses are available. The roller coaster is at the top of the hill, and the leader is at the controls.

Know the Timelines

Talking to leaders is interesting because they tend to have a very keen idea of the time lines that apply to their job and how their achievements will be measured.

Michael Critelli, chairman and former CEO of the Stamford, Connecticut–based Pitney Bowes, was asked about longevity in the top job. This was his reply: "Ten to 13 years for our size of company is optimal. If I was running GE, 20 years may be optimal—but we're not that big. You keep the succession pipeline fresh," Critelli says. "One of the risks of staying in the job for 20 years is that talented people who are a little younger and aspire to my job would leave. If they can have a reasonable tenure, I can keep them engaged and have a stronger team behind me. There is a benefit to having an orderly succession process and not staying until the board of directors forces you to leave. Beyond a certain length of time, you get to believe that you can't be replaced, so it is best to leave when you are still on top and still fresh."

Critelli went on to reflect that a friend had told him that during the first three years on the job, you're basically trying to get acclimated. During the next five or six years, you are a change agent—you put in place your programs and vision for the company. And in the last four years, you are focused on succession planning, ensuring that the talent is there for the next generation.

Adding Up to 100

Keeping these points in mind, let's consider the first 100 days and what you need to get done—and, importantly, be seen doing. Of course, many other books have their own suggestions. Some are more helpful—and humorous—than others. In their book *The Accidental Leader*, Harvey Robbins and Michael Finley offer an assessment test to establish the difficulty of the task ahead. Answer the questions, add up the scores, and discover whether the challenge is transition friendly, challenging but doable, uphill all the way, transition hostile, or Dilbertia. The first is encouraging, the last "an insane enterprise whose true product is the spiritual evisceration of its people."

I think leaders must accomplish six fundamental tasks in those first 100 days:

1. Mastering morale
2. Talking the talk
3. Assembling the team

4. Taking action

5. Writing your own legend

6. Assessing the culture and change

Mastering Morale

"The reality in my company is that 30 percent of the people do 100 percent of the work. My job is to get the other 70 percent to do something," one leader confided to me.

The morale of an organization's people is crucial at any time, but especially when a new leader takes over. In their book *The Enthusiastic Employee*, David Sirota, Louis Mischkind, and Michael Meltzer found that the stock price of companies with high morale exceeds that of similar companies in the same industries by more than 2.5 to 1; the stock price of companies with low morale lags behind their industry competitors by almost 5 to 1.

Testing an organization's morale is not difficult. Walk into any office, and you will be able to detect morale levels fairly quickly. Within minutes, you can identify those groups I pointed out earlier—the 20 percent of people ready for change, the 60 percent who are unsure, and the 20 percent stubbornly adamant that change isn't for them. Organizations have enormous built-in political and cultural inertia.

Leaders must understand a few key points about morale. First, people have a natural aspiration to be part of a winning team. The reality is that people don't change jobs because of money—60 percent of people who have left organizations cite reasons other than money for their departure. People want meaningful, enjoyable, and rewarding working experiences. Part of the leader's job is to convince people that the organization can meet their aspirations.

Second, good news exists in any organization. "It is interesting how much a single leader can set in motion," says Harvard Business School's Rosabeth Moss Kanter, who has studied turnarounds and the leadership skills required to make them happen. "In turnarounds, it is quite striking how much fresh leadership can accomplish by unlocking talent and potential which was already there in the organization but was stifled by rules, regulations, and bureaucracy." The leader *is* the good news.

Any organization has people with exceptional skills and a track record of achievement, some units are high-performing, and so on. Even if the majority of the organization is filled with unexceptional people and poorly performing units with a track record of failure, bright lights do exist. You need to quickly find them.

Getting to know people quickly is an art. This is corporate speed dating—you like him but not her, she has promise, he is trying too hard to impress. For someone in a top job, this could happen through a speech to hundreds of employees. For a team leader, it might be a chat with just a few team members. Either way, it's essential to get it right.

Talking the Talk

When I took over running the European and Asian operations of Heidrick & Struggles, I distributed those colorful bands that people wear on their wrists to remind them of some worthy cause. Mine read "Fun/Respect." For any business leader, this is the worthiest of worthy causes.

"From the first day I took over, I was communicating my expectations and the direction I wanted to go," says Ribar. "It was a matter of improving communication and letting people know I'm here." She committed herself to a lot of traveling to communicate her message and to get out and meet people. "It's worth it because of the positive feedback, and I'm learning so much. I always combine it with seeing customers, which, for me, is the only new part in my job because I have previously always managed people."

Internally, Ribar's key strategy meeting with the top management team laid the agenda clearly in front of them. "I put the team together and aligned them under one roof and behind one target. It was a question of organization: setting the target, setting the agenda for what we want to do, aligning them but also making them responsible," she says. One weakness her team identified was that they didn't implement strategy. Ribar had a message for her team: "In a year's time, if we are sitting here again saying the same thing, we have a problem. Nobody else will do it—it's our job to implement our strategy."

Sam Parker, cofounder of media company MaxPitch Media, told me that one of the first things he did when he took over as CEO was to get rid of the instant messaging in the office. Everyone thought he was crazy. They said, "How can you, a media Internet company, get rid of instant messaging?" He said, "Because no one's talking to each other." It made a huge impact on the firm's culture.

To say that communication is important to the new leader is a no-brainer. The question is how to communicate, in terms of both style and medium. Authenticity is important, and communication should fit your personal style. Some leaders enjoy getting personal—they're happy to open up and reveal aspects of their personal lives. This offers the chance to make an emotional connection—but it's also risky. Other leaders prefer to play it safe, sticking primarily to business matters.

Consider other communication advice from top leaders: Communicate in a manner that is consistent with the corporate culture. Choose settings that you are comfortable with—large crowds or small groups. Consciously monitor and adjust the signals you are sending. Reuse communications in various forums and formats to reinforce the message.

Remember, too, that everyone is watching. "Every time you walk down the hallway, you're sending a message to people," advises Skinner. "You're always saying, 'Well, what kind of message am I sending?'"

You should also remember that a new leader will not have all the answers. Asking questions and listening are important at this early stage. Don't restrict listening to insiders—try to get external perspectives, such as from customers and suppliers.

Assembling the Team

Assembling a strong team is at the top of the 100 days to-do list. As Collins said, "First who, then what." The idea that the leader comes in and picks a whole new team is just that—an idea. The reality is that new leaders need to work with the people they already have and get the best out of them, at least for the first 100 days.

Not everyone signs up for change. You need to manage them. Rose identified three types of people at M&S. First were the people who actually knew a problem existed and wanted to cure it. Second is the group you could probably persuade to recognize a problem existed. The last group refused to believe anything was wrong. Unfortunately, as is often the case, those in the third group tended to be the longer-serving people, the organization's "glue." Removing a number of board members helped convince some of the people with doubts that Rose was serious and that their jobs were at risk.

New leaders must focus on getting to know people and assessing their strengths and weaknesses. They should probe to find out how well team members know their stuff. When performing team building, think "complementary" instead of "supplementary." "I've often told people, if you have ten reports and you like them all, you've got some bad advice—you've got the wrong people on the job," says Skinner. "I always refer to my poor construction manager that I had when I was in Pittsburgh. I couldn't stand being around the guy. He'd come down the hallway; I'd go down the other way. And he was the absolute best guy to be building our buildings and doing the job for us." A team of "you" clones might be good for the ego, but it's rarely good for the organization. The memory of the predecessor will linger, as will his or her values and actions. So new leaders should be careful not to badmouth or dismiss the previous CEO in front of the team, to keep from alienating people loyal to the previous incumbent.

Finally, use the first team meetings to set the tone for those that follow. Set the style and the process.

Taking Action

Don't think vision—think priorities. Legendary CEO Lou Gerstner famously dismissed the vision thing when he set out his course of action at IBM. Gerstner was the new CEO at an ailing IBM. His job was to breathe new life into a corporate giant on the critical list. It was normal practice for CEOs to spell out their vision. But Gerstner was right to resist the temptation. As he correctly observed at the time, "The last thing IBM needs [now] is a vision." Instead, he delivered five priorities to revive the company:

1. Stop hemorrhaging cash.
2. Make sure the company is profitable by year two, inspiring confidence among the stakeholders.
3. Implement a key customer strategy to demonstrate that the company has the interests of its customers at heart.
4. Get redundancies out of the way quickly.
5. Develop an intermediate strategy.

This is simply put but difficult to execute.

New leaders should look for some easy wins to set them on their way. Quick victories in the beginning build credibility. Set priorities but don't list too many. Concentrate on a select few that will make a difference.

Rose excelled at this. "We had to find one or two places where we could demonstrate that there was traction," he says. "I've always said that women's wear is the key to the golden gate of Marks & Spencer. You want to get the key to the doors of happiness? You get that golden key that goes into women's wear. Menswear will come right, children's wear will come right, lingerie will come right, everything will come right if you get women's wear right."

But M&S also had a profitable food business. Despite the fact that food revenues were down a little, M&S had kept up its rate of innovation and maintained its value. "Women were coming in with their blinkers on, walking through the clothing department to go downstairs to the food hall, thinking 'Oh, I won't look at the clothing because the clothing's all terrible,'" says Rose. "So we had to work on women's wear first."

Kate Bostock, who now heads women's wear and lingerie at M&S, had been retained a couple months before Rose came. He gave her explicit instructions: "Your priority is to fix this. Forget about everything else—I'll worry about the shops."

At Alliance Boots, Baker identified three things he wanted to do: become a successful international business, make a contribution to the health care industry, and make people proud to work for the company.

In addition, leaders need to be inclusive. Drawing others into the strategy process will likely improve buy-in. Use a similar approach when encountering resistance. Roll with the punches, use them to your advantage, and, if possible, incorporate elements of resistance into the plan.

Writing Your Own Legend

It is commonly argued that change begins with the leader achieving some easy wins, signaling that new rules now apply. In reality, leaders can do very few easy and meaningful things that make an immediate material difference to an organization's performance. But leaders can create their own legend, to make clear through symbolic acts what matters to them and the organization. News travels fast in organizations, and it needs to work in the new hire's favor. People gauge the health of the company, the robustness of a department, the vim of a division, by looking at the leader—you are the weather vane.

For example, I heard of a banking CEO who was amazed to find that the approval process for certain loans involved getting signatures on a piece of paper from someone on the first floor, then someone else on the third floor, and, finally, the CEO. All this took time because everyone who needed to sign was extremely busy and often not in the office. Loans took three days to approve. The next time the CEO received a loan approval document, he called the other signatories into the office and told them that from then on, one signature from either of them would suffice. That wasn't rocket science, but the message was clear: Customers come first and bureaucracy must be reduced. The story speedily spread throughout the bank.

At a telecommunications company, the new boss reassigned the parking spaces outside the entrance to customers instead of to senior executives. One of Greg Dyke's first actions as the new director general of the British Broadcasting Corporation was to eliminate the chauffeur-driven cars allocated to senior executives. It sent a clear message that cost cutting started at the top of the organization instead of the bottom.

"Executives sometimes think changing the culture or getting good results from people as something that requires very elaborate, long programs," says Kanter. "But someone like Greg Dyke at the BBC started with the behavior of the 18 people who reported to him. The quality of the way people treat each other starts with the team at the top."

Assessing the Culture and Making Changes

Next on the new leader's agenda is transforming the culture of the organization, or environment, in which they are working.

"Culture isn't just one aspect of the game," says Gerstner. "It is the game, in the end. And organization is nothing more than the collective capacity of its people to create value."

To change culture, first you need to know what you are dealing with. Linked to the corporate culture should be such words as *excellence, shareholder value, integrity,* and *customer-led.* But in most companies, the culture is revealed not through words, but through actions. New leaders must read the unwritten code that the company lives by. They must interpret culture by observation and inquiry.

The actual transformation is something that the workforce does, not the leader. The leader creates the conditions for change, inviting a culture change to take place. The leader does this by instituting new operating processes, by choosing a new management team, and by leading by example.

Don't move too quickly, though. Transforming a corporate culture takes time. With too much upheaval, something will give—and it might be the leader.

Mastering the 3 Rs

An interesting story about the early days comes from Chip McClure, chairman, CEO, and president of ArvinMeritor. His approach was a good combination of listening, observing, and taking decisive action. McClure was made CEO in August 2004. One of his initial aims was to spend time one-on-one with every board member. McClure traveled extensively around the world, listening and learning. "I traveled to as many places as I could get to," he says. "I met with many of our customers, suppliers, and joint-venture partners; visited our global plants and facilities; and talked to board members, employees, and shareholders. I also spent time on Wall Street—just listening."

Then came the action, as McClure rolled out his 3R strategy to rationalize and refocus the company. "In these fast-paced times, you have to move quickly—the longer you go without doing something, the more you begin to create uncertainty," he says. "No matter what level you're at, people are looking for you to make decisions. And you have to do that with the information you've got at the time. You may have to tweak it a bit or go 5 degrees right or left, but you have to get out there. You cannot sit there and wait 6, 12, 18 months to get something done. Are you fully knowledgeable on everything at that point? The answer is no, but after spending time listening, observing, and learning, you've got to go with the best you've got. And my clear advice to anybody, almost at any level, is to and get out to as many places and meet with as many stakeholders as you can [in the first 90 or 100 days]. Absorb the information and then identify a game plan and go forward. If you need to tweak it later, do it."

This resulted in McClure's 3R strategy: rationalize, refocus, and regenerate. The rationalization element came in spring 2005 when plant closures were announced. This restructuring initiative, a $135 million endeavor involving 11 plants, was necessary to right-size the company. Then came the refocus element. During the next two years, the company focused on strengthening its core competences. The company was in too many different and noncore businesses, so it announced several divestitures. It sold its light vehicle aftermarket business and then its emissions technology business. Next came the third R: regenerate. McClure and his team identified three key areas for growth.

For the first couple years, the company spent most of its time focusing on the first two Rs. It's now focused on the regeneration strategy. However, it is still continuing to rationalize and restructure. In spring 2007, ArvinMeritor announced a second restructuring program, which will take it to the next level. "Change is a constant," says McClure. "As the industry continues to change, you can't just get locked into one thing and say 'That's it forever.' You've got to be flexible and adapt quickly to the changes in the industry." "Think, act, change" could be the new leader's mantra.

Get Lucky

Let's discuss one final element during the first 100 days and beyond. It is inexplicable and beyond management: luck. Napoleon hoped to recruit lucky generals, and so must organizations. You have no control over the vicissitudes of global markets. The best leaders maximize their influence over what matters to the organization and over the aspects of its performance they can influence. And then, hopefully, the added spice of good fortune appears.

Key Points

- It really is tough at the top. You must build success on first understanding the time frames of the process. This begins with anticipation and is followed by exploration, building, and contributing. Only fools rush in without a keen idea of the process and its associated time frames.

- A new leader must focus on six key things during the early stages:

1. **Mastering morale**—Listen to how people feel.

2. **Talking the talk**—Constantly and carefully communicate.

3. **Assembling the team**—Leadership is teamwork.

4. **Taking action**—The job is about action, but focused, deliberate action is preferable to indiscriminately doing things for the sake of doing something.

5. **Writing your own legend**—Symbolic actions can shape your entire tenure.

6. **Assessing the culture and making changes**—Any change must involve understanding and changing the corporate culture.

- Finally, wish for good fortune.

Resources

Bruch, Heike, and Sumantra Ghoshal. "Management Is the Art of Doing and Getting Done." *Business Strategy Review* 15 (Autumn 2004): 4–13.

McGregor, Jena. "How to Take the Reins at Top Speed." *Business Week*, 5 February, 2007.

Ciampa, Dan, and Michael Watkins. *Right From the Start*. (Boston: Harvard Business School Press, 1999.)

Gerstner, Lou. *Who Says Elephants Can't Dance?* (New York: Collins, 2002.)

Kanter, Rosabeth Moss. *Confidence*. (Boston: Harvard Business School Press, 2006.)

Robbins, Harvey, and Michael Finley. *The Accidental Leader*. (San Francisco: Jossey-Bass, 2003.)

Sirota, David, Louis Mischkind, and Michael Meltzer. *The Enthusiastic Employee*. (Upper Saddle River: Wharton Publishing, 2005.)

Trapp, Roger. "Turnarounds—A Turn for the Better." *Financial Director*, 23 May 2005.

Watkins, Michael. *The First 90 Days*. (Boston: Harvard Business School Press, 2003.)

4

The Job: Leadership, Strategy, and Execution

Every top job begins with leadership. You are in charge. But where are you leading your people, and how can you ensure they get there? Without strategy and execution, leadership is decorative.

> "You don't become a leader without followers. You only know if you have followers when you ask them to do something really difficult and they do it with enthusiasm."
>
> —*Richard Baker, CEO, Alliance Boots*

Who's in Charge?

Gerry Roche, senior chairman of Heidrick & Struggles, tells the story of how Bill Paley, founder of the CBS Corporation and the Tiffany Network, brought him in. At the time, CBS was the leading broadcasting organization in the world, and Paley was the equivalent of Rupert Murdoch. Paley brought Roche in to find his successor. After the company went public, the board had directed Paley to bring in a chief operating officer as the anointed successor. Roche recruited Tom Wyman, who was the chairman and CEO of Green Giant in the Midwest. Wyman was an extraordinarily impressive candidate. "He looked like Gary Cooper, just the quintessence of the top CEO—he'd sit on the cover of *Fortune* beautifully," Roche recalls.

When Paley interviewed Wyman, he thought he was a perfect candidate and wanted to make him an offer. The trouble was that Paley had a record of hiring COOs for a year or two and then firing them. So Wyman told Roche that he wouldn't touch the job unless Paley made him CEO. "I went back to Paley, this huge man with his huge ego and a huge reputation, and I told him that Tom Wyman wouldn't come unless Paley made him CEO. And he said, 'COO, CEO—who gives a damn as long as everybody knows who's boss around here?'"

Roche recounts this story for a simple reason: to show that whatever words or definitions you use, the essential role of the CEO is to lead, inspire, and take responsibility. He explains: "You can play with titles and structures, but the fundamental question is, who's running the show? And that's the definition in my book of the CEO: the person who is responsible for successfully running the entire operation. That's what the CEO is responsible for: the strategy, the execution, the hiring of people, the legal function, the HR function, and, to the extent that he designs the structure under him, where he divides it into operations and support and public exposure jobs. I have difficulty coming up with some nice McKinsey or Harvard definition for the job description of a CEO. The bottom line is that the CEO is the person who's responsible to the shareholders for running the firm, and he is responsible to the board of directors who are responsible for picking the CEO. It's that simple."

Having a top job isn't about a job title, a large office, or a parking space. When he took over as CEO of Alliance Boots, Richard Baker moved into an open-plan office instead of the traditional CEO's office. "Businesses are run by teams, and I have a team of 100,000. I may have the captain's armband on, but I am like everyone else." Indeed, Baker tries to keep himself grounded with others in his company. "I don't need a lot of status—too much status means that people won't talk to you," he says. On his first day, Baker was given a name badge, as all the company's employees are. It said "Mr. R. A. Baker, Chief Executive." He asked for it to be changed simply to "Richard."

The Objectives

You have the title. You have the badge with your name. You might even have a parking space with your name on it. But what are you expected to achieve in a top job? What are the key performance measures? Not surprisingly, opinions vary on this topic. "The bigger the company is, the more the job is really managing the people, putting the right people at the right place, thinking about the future of the company, trying to bring everything under one roof, and setting the strategy," says Monika Ribar of Panalpina.

For me, the following three key considerations keep employees happy, engaged, and loyal to the company, and these constitute the underlying objectives in everything that I do:

1. *Interest in what they do*—This could be marketing, finance, consulting, or whatever.
2. *Compensation*—This involves not just what people are paid and their bonuses, but also how fairly people are treated.
3. *Learning*—When candidates approach us as a search firm, it is usually because they feel they have stopped learning and developing in their current firm.

As my colleagues and I look for the leaders of the future, we find ourselves coming back to that third point—learning—as the most critical. Generation Y'ers (those born between 1977 and 2005) will have an average of 14 jobs by the time they are 38. I believe that the organizations that will succeed in the long term are those that provide their employees with the right learning opportunities. As a leader, I hope I never stop learning, and when I'm promoting people or looking for future leaders within my firm, I look closely at how they encourage, develop, and train the talent below them. Few tests are more effective at predicting leadership potential.

According to leadership thinker Warren Bennis, these are the key performance indicators:

1. Does alignment exist in the organization? Does the company have a collectively shared definition of success that's understood and rewarded throughout the organization?

2. Does the organization display adaptive capacity or resilience? Can it foresee and adapt to continual change—without the habit of success getting in the way? Samuel Beckett's play *Waiting for Godot* has a great line in which Didi, one of the two tramps, says to the other tramp, Gogo, "Habit is a great deadener." Successful habits are even more of a deadener.

3. How is the organization performing financially? Whether it's market capitalization, return on investment, the success of acquisitions or divestitures—whatever the company is using as its measure of financial success must be evaluated.

4. Does the organization develop a bench—a cadre—of future leaders? Does it mentor future leaders?

5. Does the workforce feel motivated, empowered, animated, and engaged?

6. Is the organization relatively open—does it have transparency?

7. What amount of resources is the organization allocating to future research and development?

Beyond Charisma

You can't argue with much of Bennis's summary. Most jobs come with a job description, a lengthy list of the exact parameters of responsibility. But as you approach the top, the job descriptions gradually fizzle out. With top jobs, the job titles—whether you are a CTO, CMO, CHRO, or CEO—are as riddled with ambiguity as they are resonant with corporate status. You are largely left alone to make it up as you go along, which can be good or bad.

The loneliness can be hard: You wake up and realize you have become the person you used to complain about. Compared with the experience of most executives, the leader has enormous freedom—to choose what to do, when, and with whom. Previously, I had been an executive cocooned in routine and certainty; as a leader, I realized uncertainty rules.

Phil Hodgson, coauthor of the aptly titled *Relax, It's Only Uncertainty*, sees the lack of control as the greatest challenge for anyone in a top job. "The leader faces uncertainty outside the organization in the form of expectations about organizational performance, direction, and, if appropriate, stock price. But the leader also faces uncertainty inside the organization in the form of managerial performance, operational effectiveness, and realization of human potential," he says. "The role of the leader is, therefore, to choose the areas of uncertainty where the strategic challenges will be met externally and support the areas of learning where the managerial challenges will be met internally."

Leaders must learn to revel in the uncertainty, the ambiguity offered by the job. "Management is a science, but being a CEO is an art," former Toshiba CEO Taizo Nishimura once reflected.

And you need to be an artist of every medium. "I think the CEO has three jobs or roles," says Barry Gibbons, former chairman and CEO of Burger King and now an author and consultant. "First, to have 'The Dream' (this is *not* a mission or a mission statement). It is Bill Gates seeing a PC on every table. Second, the CEO is all about *how* you do business, less about what you do. It is the style factors. What do you stand for? What do you stand by? What are the imperatives? What's the balance of the company? Are you responsive or deaf? Backbone or invertebrate? Third, the CEO is the leader figure, watched by a whole range of audiences. This is not about style versus substance; it's about understanding how you *personally* can best impact the first two roles. What are the key audiences—Wall Street? Consumers?

Lobby groups? Your employees? Unions? Get involved personally and show them what you and the company stand for."

Jacques Aigrain, CEO of Swiss Re, offered another take on the role. Swiss Re is the world's largest reinsurance group. When I spoke to Aigrain, Swiss Re's profits had just doubled, and its net income stood at $3.8 billion. Aigrain took over as CEO in early 2006, after a spell as deputy CEO. He started his career with JP Morgan in 1981. "A large majority of people don't really understand what a CEO does. Even within your own company, most people do not know how the CEO's time is spent," he says. "In my case, I had a huge number of tactical issues to deal with in the first year. Then as more time has passed, I'm looking forward to see what the strategy should be, what the key challenges are in the longer term."

The One-Word Job Description

If you could pick one word to sum up any top job, it is *leadership*.

Some people confuse leadership with charisma. In the New Testament, "charisms" were gifts that the Holy Spirit bestowed. People with charisma in this sense include good leaders, but they are also those with the ability to perform miracles or speak in tongues. We often expect leaders to perform miracles, and sometimes they speak in tongues.

Charismatic leaders loom large in history. They include Napoleon, Churchill, and Gandhi. In more recent times, charisma has become synonymous with secular success. "Charisma wasn't always important in business," notes Rakesh Khurana, an associate professor at Harvard Business School. "For three decades following World War II, the typical chief executive was an organization man who worked his way up the ranks."

According to Khurana, that started to change in 1979 with the appointment of Lee Iaccoca as CEO of Chrysler. "Iacocca was inspirational in a way that previous business leaders had not been," Khurana says. "His successful turnaround of Chrysler made him a national hero in America and ushered in the era of the charismatic CEO."

Jack Welch at GE, Steve Jobs at Apple Computer, and Richard Branson at Virgin are all examples of charismatic business leaders. They radiate a personal magnetism that attracts employees and customers alike. But how much of that aura comes from their position as leader?

A lot, according to Manfred Kets de Vries, a professor with INSEAD. "It's a fantasy," he says. "People project their expectations onto the leader. But if you want to stimulate a fantasy, you can do a few things. It helps if you are a good orator. It helps if you can tell stories and use imagery. It helps if you have a good memory for names. It helps if you are attentive and people at least have the illusion that you listen to them—what I call the teddy bear factor. It also helps if you are willing to ask questions and challenge the status quo."

Charismatic leaders also rely on symbol manipulation. In ancient times, leaders often wore special clothing, masks, and ornaments to appear larger than life, notes Khurana. Kings and queens assume charisma through their family heritage. For the modern business leader, private jets, limousines, palatial homes, and the other trappings of corporate power perform the same function.

At this point, the dangers of charisma become apparent. Bernie Ebbers at WorldCom and Dennis Kozlowski at Tyco were both charismatic leaders. The collapse of Enron was also fuelled by a heady cocktail of charisma and greed. Right up until the very end, former CEO Jeffrey Skilling and CFO Andrew Fastow continued to charm investors and analysts at gatherings that one insider likened to revival meetings.

The point is that charisma can blind people to the failings of individuals or their arguments. This is causing a reappraisal among leadership experts. Jeffrey Garten, dean of the Yale School of Management and author of *The Politics of Fortune: A New Agenda for Business Leadership*, argues that an important task for today's leaders is to redefine the character of leadership. "Much of the past decade was about the swaggering and self-promoting CEO," he notes, "but it would be a misreading of current and future requirements if business leaders concluded that charisma is a bad thing. Indeed, it is a trait that is part and parcel of effective leadership at any time."

So charisma is not the be-all and end-all of leadership. I know plenty of leaders who are not charismatic, but they are certainly leaders.

Celebrity leaders do not always add value. Jack Welch, Steve Jobs, Louis Gerstner, Bill Gates, Larry Ellison, Andrew Grove, and Carly Fiorina are just some of the leaders (and ex-leaders) who have had celebrity status conferred on them by the business media. Interestingly, many leaders I talk to are uncomfortable with this trend. They don't want to be celebrities; they want to run great organizations. "There is a worrying trend of celebratization," laments Baker. "Business reporting is much more personalized. There are fewer stories about companies. People have very unrealistic expectations of leaders."

The question must be what impact "star" leaders actually have. Four business researchers examined the results of the *Financial World* CEO of the Year contest between 1992 and 1997 to see whether they or their companies benefited from their fame. The study covered 278 companies from the S&P 500, collecting data on total CEO compensation and company performance—both changes in share price in the days immediately after the rankings were published and market returns (total change in share price for the year). They then tested the sample to see the effect of CEO star status, comparing how the firms with celebrity leaders performed against the average stock market performance and, more specifically, against market expectations for that firm.

The findings showed an initial positive effect for the organization. For the firm, an immediate uptick in share price followed the announcement of the winners of the CEO contest. This leads to a slight rise in market return—against both the average and the individual expectation—which is most pronounced the day after the results are announced (up about 0.25 percent). But this effect soon faded as the information was integrated into investors' evaluation of the firm, contributing to higher expectations of those firms led by star leaders. Compared with these elevated hopes, the results quickly turned negative. Within 30 days, the effect on expected market return for the firm versus actual market return became marginally negative, and it became significantly negative during the following eight months.

Meanwhile, the CEO benefits during both the short and the long term. "Winning a medal in the current year increases a CEO's pay by approximately 10 percent," the authors note, "and each medal awarded in the previous five years adds almost five percent to his/her pay."

The findings suggest that boards expect higher performance from their star leaders and reward them accordingly. Similarly, analysts expect star leaders to deliver superior results to those of their less famous peers and raise their hopes. But no clear evidence exists that their confidence is justified. In fact, firm performance often fails to live up to these higher expectations. So even though the celebrity leaders might not perform any better or any worse than average, their celebrity status means that they are rewarded with above-average compensation (compared with nonwinning leaders). This suggests that paying over-the-odds compensation to attract stars is a risky strategy.

So if celebrity is not a useful measure of efficacy, what is?

The Meaning of Leadership

Executive leaders are usually judged on financial results. But another equally important aspect of leadership exists: providing meaning.

Research by Joel Podolny, Novartis Professor of Leadership and Management; Rakesh Khurana, an associate professor; and Marya Hill-Popper, a doctoral student at Harvard Business School, suggests that leadership impacts meaning in several ways. First, leaders make architectural choices—how to structure the organization, design jobs, and allocate roles and responsibilities—that shape how people who work in the organization experience their jobs. Second, leaders engage in symbolic actions—through the stories they tell, the symbols and rituals they create, and other highly visible actions. The leader is both architect and visionary, and both roles impact the meaning that individuals experience through work.

So what is the connection between meaning-making capacity and economic performance? Podolny and his coauthors offer two answers. The first, as they admit, is a defiant one. "One of the most significant problems with the study of organizations is that the concern with economic outcomes has trumped the concern with other outcomes. Satisfaction, meaning, social welfare—all seem to be regarded as secondary importance."

The researchers do not believe that establishing a connection is essential. Instead they assert that the meaningfulness of actions is important enough in its own right without establishing a connection with economic performance.

But they also acknowledge that this is not an entirely satisfactory answer. Even if one accepts that meaning is of paramount importance, it cannot be sustained to the complete exclusion of a focus on performance—because the organization will not survive.

Nor should we assume that causality flows entirely from meaning to performance. Just as it is reasonable to assume that individuals perform better when they find their work meaningful, better economic performance could have a positive impact on the meaning individuals derive from their work. Even if we ultimately find that meaning creation does not have a significant impact on performance, Podolny and his coauthors maintain that greater attention should be given to meaning. Meaning creation is too important to be subordinated to economic performance.

The conclusion? "Meaning creation is an important phenomenon regardless of its relation to economic performance," say the Harvard experts. "Indeed, we can think of no other phenomenon that is more worthy of explanation."

For business leaders, providing meaning is as important as impacting performance.

The Magical Ingredients

The amazing thing about leadership (and plenty of people have studied it—more than 2,000 books on leadership are published every year) is that the ingredients of effective leadership remain elusive. "A leader is a dealer in hope," Napoleon once observed.

Current thinking on leadership reflects recent experience. In particular, widespread discontent surrounds a particular sort of heroic (or narcissistic) leadership, which many believe contributed to such corporate scandals as Enron, Tyco, and Vivendi.

Viewed more positively, what do I consider the essential ingredients for leadership? First, leaders are only as good as their followers. I heard a story about the founder of an international chain of hotels whose measure of success was whether the maid cleaning a room in one of the chain's farthest outposts neatly turned up the toilet paper. This is a very small thing to consider in a huge international operation, but it is built around realizing that if leaders are doing their job well, they should be having an impact on everyone in the organization.

When I spoke with H. Patrick Swygert, he was president of Howard University, a job he had held since 1995. Soon afterward, he announced his intention to leave the post in June 2008. Swygert had studied law at Howard and was previously the president at the University of Albany. Along the way, he taught throughout the world; he has been on the board of Fannie Mae, United Technologies, the Hartford Financial Services Group, and the CIA's External Advisory Board.

"You can be a great leader, or at least have the attributes of a great leader, and have no followers," Patrick observed. "How often have we seen people who, at least on paper, fit the profile, but they just can't get people to work and walk with them? I would say that comes about for two reasons. One, some believe they can act without the advice or input of others. They believe they know everything or know as much, or more, than anyone in the room. They tend to only half listen, and people pick up on that very, very quickly.

"Second, some people don't have that kind of all-encompassing, far-reaching intelligence. They're intelligent in one way, but not intelligent enough to let other people have something to say and a piece of the outcome. I think that's one of the reasons why some otherwise brilliant people can't do anything but lead themselves to the restrooms." (On a similar theme, one amazed new leader told me, "People do actually follow you to the bathroom.")

Quiet Leadership

The second key to understanding leadership is that humility outperforms charisma. In his book, *Good to Great*, Jim Collins examines how a good company becomes an exceptional company. The book introduces a new term to the leadership lexicon: Level 5 leadership. Level 5 refers to the highest level in a hierarchy of executive capabilities. Leaders at the other four levels might be successful, but they are unable to elevate companies from mediocrity to sustained excellence.

Level 5 leadership challenges the assumption that transforming companies from good to great requires larger-than-life leaders. The leaders that came out on top in Collins's five-year study were relatively unknown outside their industries. The findings appear to signal a shift of emphasis away from the hero to the antihero. According to Collins, humility is a key ingredient of Level 5 leadership. His simple formula is Humility + Will = Level 5. "The central dimension for Level 5 is a leader who is ambitious first and foremost for the cause, the company, and the work, not for himself or herself; and who has an absolutely terrifying iron will to make good on that ambition," says Collins. "It is that combination, the fact that it's not about them—it's for the company and its long-term interests, of which they are just a part. But it's not a meekness, a weakness, or a wallflower type. It's the other side of the coin."

Balancing IQ and EQ

The third key ingredient of leadership is sensitivity. Dan Goleman's book *Primal Leadership* makes the case for cultivating emotionally intelligent leaders. In it, Goleman and coauthors Richard E. Boyatzis and Annie McKee explore how the four domains of emotional intelligence—self-awareness, self-management, social awareness, and relationship management—give rise to different styles of leadership. These constitute a leadership repertoire that enlightened leaders can master to maximize their effectiveness.

I believe that the ability to balance IQ (intelligence quotient) and EQ (emotional quotient) is integral to leadership and sits at the heart of any top job. Leaders now require a broad spectrum of knowledge. The best leaders are adept at applying their analytical skills and their emotional skills at the right times. They aren't purely "people" people—they can also make sense of complex market data and strategic plans. The important characteristic is that they are able to balance the two elements.

"You can't be a dictator or someone who listens to everyone," reflects Michael Critelli, chairman of Pitney Bowes. "You have to balance stakeholders and make independent judgments. People put you in the job to represent the collective will of the organization, not to respond to every fad and fashion of the moment."

Another leader I talked to said it this way: "The problem is that you think that everyone thinks like you. But if they thought like you, they wouldn't need you as their leader."

Rob Goffee and Gareth Jones, two professors at the London Business School, emphasize the need for balance in their book *Why Should Anyone Be Led By You?* Goffee and Jones argue that effective leaders consciously move between being close to and distant from the people they lead. "The leader's job is to look out for all the stakeholders in an organization, and that can't be done if the leader is too close to any one group of them," they say. "Mired in a complex situation, the leader must rise above it to understand it. Preserving distance may be the only way to see the full picture. When establishing goals, objectives, and the rules of the game, distance is essential. Norms, values, and standards need to be communicated as nonnegotiable. These are the bedrock on which operations are built. This can only be done effectively early in a leadership relationship, with as much distance and formality as possible."

Of course, as Goffee and Jones point out, leaders can sometimes be too distant. As director general of the BBC, John Birt was renowned for his distance—so much so that when he announced a major reorganization, it came as news to everyone except the board and the team of consultants who had come up with the plan. Contrast this approach with that of Birt's successor, Greg Dyke, who was a master of closeness. Successful leaders flit easily and consciously between the two modes.

Vision and Strategy

Gerry Roche emphasizes the rarity of discovering an individual who possesses both vision and planning, and the ability to execute:

Says Roche, "I was in the navy for some time. On the bridge of a ship, you've got the captain, and then you have the executive officer, who is the second in command. The captain decides where we're going, what ports we have to make, what part of the battle plan we're going to be in, what part of the fleet we're in, and where we are going. The executive officer is the guy that he turns to and says, 'All right, now get this damn ship there and do what's been planned.' You have to boil this down to its simplest elements. Two functions are performed in every corporation: planning and doing, or vision and execution. The talents for doing those jobs, in general, are not the same. The idea that the COO's job is the natural path to becoming CEO is often assumed but is not always the case. Skills for doing and executing are not always found, nor do they necessarily lead to skills in vision and planning. Special attention needs to be given to the danger that this unwarranted assumption could lead to putting the wrong person in the CEO role. Executives who do both well do, indeed, exist. But they are rare and, ultimately, the real stars in succession planning."

I think we can all accept that leadership is at the core of being in a top job. The next two elements, the ability to create strategy and execute it, are more complicated because they tend not to be evident in the same person. As Roche points out, you are asking a lot of any one individual leader to be able to dream and to deliver.

But that is what leaders have to do. Although the COO takes care of the operational nitty-gritty, it is the CEO's job to create and implement a vision and strategy—the desired destination. "The CEO must have a vision," says Seung-Yu Kim, CEO of Hana Financial Group. "The business environment is going to change over the next five to ten years, and [CEOs] need to communicate that to their people. Preparing for the future now is a key role for the CEO."

Karan Bilimoria, founder of Cobra beer, points to a similar need for leadership: "[Chief executives need] to have a vision, to display a certain confidence to show that they are somebody who is looking ahead, who knows where they are going and where the company is going, and that they have that confidence and the faith that inspires others to go with them on that journey."

Beginning with Change

Vision is not the sole preserve of the CEO. Top jobs are always driven by change. Change must begin with a vision. "You cannot make a change or even engage in a process of change if at the beginning you do not know where you want to go," Carlos Ghosn told me. "Establishing the destination, establishing the purpose is fundamental. If you do not have a purpose, do not even try to make any changes because they will fail. Having from the beginning a clear vision, a clear sense of purpose, is fundamental to any change."

Ghosn knows from his own experience the importance of having a common goal in mind: "Prior to 1999, Nissan was a company in disarray. Company objectives were set, and people worked hard to achieve them, but then the course kept changing. People lost a sense of motivation and did not know where to go. When I came on board in 1999, my sole objective was very simple: It was to revive Nissan. This objective would determine all our priorities. It would determine even the people we would count on to achieve them. We could not compromise that goal, and nothing that could threaten the revival of the company would be accepted. What was true then is still true today. If you do not have a shared and attractive destination, you can forget about any process of change."

Many leaders spend their first 100 days, or longer, cogitating on what the vision and strategy might be. This is—or can be—incredibly valuable for the individual and the long-term health of the organization.

"During the first 100 days, people doubted my ideas. But after talking to a lot of people in those first 100 days, I created my vision," says Takeshi Niinami, CEO of Lawson. "People doubted that it could be done. People didn't believe me. But talking about the same things consistently for three years made people start to believe. And now what's happening is in line with my vision. Sometimes you have to change implementation depending on the competitive situation. But having a very simple vision and very consistent message is important. Perhaps people thought I was stupid because I was always saying the same things, but, in a sense, I wanted to brainwash people."

Swygert identifies the failure to develop a vision as a characteristic of those who fail to make the leap to truly significant leadership. "One reason why otherwise ostensibly great leaders, at least in terms of credentials and stature, are unable to lead is because they are unable either to articulate or to fashion a vision, a sense of purpose that people really can rally around. They may know where they're going, but they can't quite get it over to other people."

Execute

At some point, it has to happen. Execution is central to a top job. Sometimes companies and their leaders need to hold their breath and just jump. Going back is not an option. Executing on a plan is often preferable to cogitating about potential new plans or changing the plan midstream. "There is no plan B," confessed Stuart Rose when I spoke to him. "I remember telling the chairman in quite the same way about this, saying, 'Well, look, if I can't fix the business, don't ask me if I have an alternative plan. I haven't got one. I've only got one plan, and we're just going to keep going at this, guys, until either I get sacked or I'm proved right. There ain't no turning, we're not moving left or right. That's the way, that's going to pay off, and I won't change the plan now.'"

You might think that the capacity to act positively and purposefully is obvious. It is, but it is equally rare. Research by Heike Bruch and Sumantra Ghoshal found that only 10 percent of executives fall into the category of being full of purposeful action. Of the rest, two-fifths fall into the category of "distracted managers." They might be full of energy and highly motivated, but they also rapidly switch from one task to another, an activity described as firefighting. They spend their days flitting from meeting to meeting not knowing what they want to make happen. They're too busy to see impending problems.

Firefighting lacks any strategic imperative; consequently, distracted managers are unable to lead others. Unfortunately, many organizations have cultures that support this type of behavior. Strategy guru Henry Mintzberg spent time analyzing senior executives at work. He found that managers were slaves to the moment, moving from task to task, with every move dogged by another diversion or telephone call. The median time spent on any one issue was a mere nine minutes. (Mintzberg's work was published in 1973, so email, mobile phones, and other devices have likely reduced this number even further.)

I have learned to separate what is urgent versus what is important, and that comes down to judgment. My years in executive search have shown me that the leaders who fail are those who micromanage and overcomplicate everything, who are convinced they must be involved in every detail. I am curious about everything but realize I cannot be an expert in every single area of our business; I have to rely on the expertise of others. If you have the right people in place, this is not hard because you trust those people to tell you what is crucial. They then grow and develop because they know they have your support—we all know how good it feels to be relied on.

Bruch and Ghoshal also calculate that another 30 percent of executives are procrastinators. "They can't even get started," says Bruch. "Experience has taught them that whatever they do won't make any difference to anything. They certainly can't motivate others." The remaining 20 percent are disengaged. These people are focused but not driven or excited by what they do. They lack the energy to deal with problems or to drive things through.

The problem is that many managers confuse being active with being productive. They become too absorbed with routine tasks and firefighting, leaving little time or energy for issues requiring reflection, systematic planning, or creative thinking. One leader I talked to kept Friday clear on his calendar so that he could deal with the things that emerged during the week or even, unusually, to get ahead. It worked for him.

"Action demands energy," explains Bruch. "Some managers fail to take purposeful action simply because they lack energy. Some are exhausted or burned out from stress and do not have the inner resources to reenergize themselves. For others, the lack of energy may be relevant to a particular project that is not meaningful to them. Without energy, they are unable to go the extra mile that is often necessary to accomplish nonroutine tasks." Focus, on the other hand, involves concentrated attention, she says. "It is the ability to zero in on a goal and see it successfully through to completion."

Key Points

- Top job descriptions are the subject of continuing debate, but everyone agrees that they are wide ranging. At their heart lies leadership.
- The contemporary practice of leadership has progressed from the historical command-and-control model. Leadership is not solely about charisma, although being charismatic helps. Instead, leadership must be based on understanding the needs of followers, exhibiting humility instead of ego, and being able to balance EQ and IQ.
- Leaders must master execution—purposeful action. Their actions must be carefully focused and their energies channeled into acting at the right time in the right way.
- Leaders are responsible for generating and living the company's vision and for creating and implementing strategy.

Resources

Badaracco Jr., J. "We Don't Need Another Hero." *Harvard Business Review* 79.8 (September 2001): 120–26; 162.

Bennis, Warren. "The Seven Ages of the Leader." *Harvard Business Review* 82.1 (January 2004): 46–53; 112.

Bilimoria, Karan. *Bottled for Business* (Chichester, UK: Capstone Press, 2007).

Bruch, Heike, and Sumantra Ghoshal. "Management Is the Art of Doing and Getting Done." *Business Strategy Review* 15 (September 2004): 4–13.

Collins, James. "Level 5 Leadership: The Triumph of Humility and Fierce Resolve." *Harvard Business Review* 79.1 (January 2001): 66–75; 175.

Collins, Jim. *Good to Great* (New York: HarperBusiness, 2001).

Collins, Jim, and Jerry I. Porras. *Built to Last: Successful Habits of Visionary Companies* (New York: HarperBusiness, 1995).

Conger, Jay, and Rabindra Kanungo. *Charismatic Leadership in Organizations* (Thousand Oaks, California: Sage, 1998).

Dearlove, Des. "Leading from the Top: An Interview with Warren Bennis." EFMD Thought Leader Series, www.efmd.org.

Dvorak, John C. "Too Many Chiefs." *PC Magazine*, October 2002.

Garten, Jeffrey. *The Politics of Fortune: A New Agenda for Business Leadership* (Boston: Harvard Business School Press, 2002).

Goffee, Rob, and Gareth Jones. "Why Should Anyone Be Led by You?" *Harvard Business Review* 78.5 (September-October, 2000): 62–70; 198.

Goffee, Rob, and Gareth Jones. *Why Should Anyone Be Led By You?* (Boston: Harvard Business School Press, 2006).

Goleman, Daniel. *Emotional Intelligence* (New York: Bantam, 1995).

Goleman, Daniel, and Richard Boyatzis. *Primal Leadership* (Boston: Harvard Business School Press, 2002).

Hodgson, Phil, and Randall P. White. *Relax, It's Only Uncertainty* (London: FT Prentice Hall, 2004).

Mintzberg, Henry. *The Nature of Managerial Work* (New York: Harper & Row, 1973).

Podolny, Joel, Rakesh Khurana, and Marya Hill-Popper. "Revisiting the Meaning of Leadership." *Research in Organizational Behavior* 26 (2005): 1–37.

PricewaterhouseCoopers. *9th Annual Global CEO Survey*. 2006.

5

The Job: Communication and People

How do you convince people that you are the person to provide leadership, that your strategy is the right one, and that execution relies on everyone contributing? Only connect.

"You have to be curious. What is going on? If you just sit in your office, I don't think that you can do the job like that, and I don't think that you can do it in the future."

—*Monika Ribar, CEO, Panalpina*

Elevator Pitch

Tim Flynn, chairman of KPMG International and chairman and CEO of KPMG LLP, its U.S. member firm, has a disarming openness—and it led me to think about how powerful and persuasive it must be for insiders. First, he talked about whether he was the right man for the job. "I'm not the only person in my firm who can do this job," he told me. "I'm the only person who can do it the way that *I* do it, because everyone is unique in how they carry out these responsibilities." His viewpoint holds that certain people are suited for certain jobs in an organization at certain times; the key is managing the right person with the right skill set at the right time.

Flynn argues that the higher you progress up the leadership hierarchy, the broader your span of accountability is. In other words, you can get involved in many more things as you climb the leadership ladder. This poses two questions: How good are you at delegating? And for what do you arrange your time so you can get involved?

One thing Flynn doesn't delegate is something he patently enjoys: reaching out directly to people in the organization. "The time I enjoy the most is [being] out in front of our people," he says. Flynn attends orientation for the company's 1,000 new hires, and he goes to the annual partners meeting to talk to the partners one-on-one. Within the company, he frequently pops into people's offices to say hi and ask what they're doing. Afterward he gets emails saying no one else in a leadership position ever did that. "The impact you have on people and the ability to bring faith to an organization is powerful," Flynn says.

At KPMG's New York headquarters on Park Avenue, the firm has a number of floors. This means there's a high probability that anyone in the elevator is from KPMG. If he's in the elevator, Flynn keeps his eyes open. If someone pushes the number for one of KPMG's floors, he asks if they're with KPMG and then introduces himself. Naturally, the employees are usually shocked. Flynn simply goes on to ask about their roles in the company and have "great conversations" with them. "That sort of thing buzzes around the organization, and you can see the impact," he says. Indeed, think of the impact on a company from a chairman who is passionate about engaging with people and who takes every opportunity to do so.

Constantly Communicating

"Communication is an ongoing and huge challenge in any organization, particularly when change is happening," says Peter Sharpe, president and CEO of Cadillac Fairview Corporation. "During restructuring, I took it upon myself to do daily recordings so people could call in, and I'd do phone calls to the entire company on a regular basis. We'd send out updates on everything that was going on, and it was never enough—you just cannot overcommunicate."

If leadership is the job, making this happen demands communication. Anyone worth his or her salt in a top job constantly communicates; these leaders connect authentically, powerfully, and persuasively with people. (Note the word *authentically*.)

I like the Dilbert cartoon in which the boss approaches the long-suffering technical writer and announces that he has decided to write a daily blog. "Every day I will record my personal thoughts about our business," he declares. Then he adds, "I need you to write the first one by noon. I can't wait to see what I'm thinking!"

We can all share the writer's dismay. Communication, whether by blog or by more traditional means, is not something a leader can delegate. Of course, leaders need help with communication, but the sentiments communicated should always be their own, whether the news is good or bad.

Consider Jim Skinner, vice chairman and CEO of McDonald's since 2004. He served nearly ten years in the U.S. Navy before beginning his career with McDonald's in 1971 as a restaurant manager trainee in Carpentersville, Illinois. Through his career, he has held numerous top jobs. For Skinner, it doesn't matter whether you're running a restaurant or a corporation—it all boils down to communication. "I think the important thing, in the best of times and in the worst of times, is communicating a clear vision for the organization," he told me. "This leads to strategic intent—tactics and all those other kinds of things—but most importantly, it is about who we are and what we stand for." Skinner emphasizes that, being in the food business, McDonald's must focus on the customer. "It all revolves around doing a better job today at what we have always done," he says. "We don't do anything else that can impact the interface with our customer that makes money, anywhere in the world, except at the front counter and drive-through. Fifty-five million times a day, this is critical. It is about staying the course. We're a brand that deserves to be trusted. And the good news is the communication doesn't change whether we're in good times, or we're under heavy scrutiny, or there are issues."

Skinner's communication mantra is that less is more. He uses a BlackBerry but only because he doesn't want to carry a laptop. He uses it just to stay current on emails, information, and sales, not necessarily to communicate with people on important issues. "But you have to be accessible, and I am accessible—people can reach out for me," he says.

At Heidrick & Struggles, we produced a book of parables called *Listen*. Many of our consultants have framed one page that I particularly like on their office walls: "As a partner and consultant, you should follow your biological setup. Two ears and one mouth means listen twice as much as you talk." I think that's a pretty good maxim for any leader.

"Leaders often fail not because of lack of strategic thinking, but [because of] a lack of coherent thought about [implementing] and mobilizing the organization," says Gurnek Bains, managing director of the business psychology consultancy YSC and one of the authors of *Meaning, Inc.* "It really is about people." Bains says that before they become leaders, managers usually understand this intellectually, but only when they actually do the job do they tend to understand it emotionally. Typically, leaders spend 40 to 50 percent of their time communicating with people, Bains estimates. They also spend a surprising amount of time thinking about the top talent in the company, building teams, and attracting talented people.

Gerry Roche, senior chairman at Heidrick & Struggles, is equally clear: "The very definition of management is getting good work from others, not doing it yourself. How can you get work done through others if you aren't a good communicator or if you don't have good human sensitivities? Those are the two skills that ring my bell. Whether it's COO or CEO, you are not going to be measured on what you do yourself; you are going to be judged on the team that you build, enthuse, motivate, integrate, assess, compensate; you are going to be measured on what that team does. And what it takes to build and run a team is mainly communicating skills, human sensitivity, a bias for action, and good judgment."

The reality is that better communications could—and perhaps should—sort out most of the day-to-day problems in organizations. Poor communication is the consistent downfall of organizations, both current and future. Effective leaders constantly communicate. Indeed, they often communicate exactly the same message, but to different audiences. An appetite for repetition is part of any top job description. And the repetition must be consistent, for there is danger in varying the message, even slightly, for different audiences. If we send a message to our employees in one region, the global grapevine immediately kicks in, and soon it is all over the company: The message must be the same for all.

The need to communicate is particularly acute in troubled times. But it is a constant feature of the leader's job, no matter what stage the leader is in. Asked about how he spent his time as CEO, Pitney Bowes' Michael Critelli estimated that he spent around 5 percent on board and corporate governance matters; 25 to 30 percent on meetings (individually with people who worked with him, in staff meetings, and in around 150 one-to-one meetings every year with people from all levels of the organization); 5 to 10 percent meeting with industry officials, politicians, and other regulators; and 10 to 15 percent in some form of interaction with customers. In addition, he allocated around five days a year to talking to shareholders, analysts, and rating agencies; he split his remaining time on a variety of outside activities that somehow relate to his job. Whatever the split, communicating with people inside and outside the organization lies at the heart of the job description.

From Day One

As we have seen, communication starts on day one and is integral to creating any momentum for change. In addition to being a great communicator, Tim Flynn is one of the most change-focused leaders I have ever met. A 28-year veteran of KPMG, Flynn started his career in the firm's Minneapolis office in 1979. So how did it feel to reach the top of the organization? "When you become a leader in an organization, it's all about earning the right to have other people trust you as a leader and then recognize the responsibility and the accountability that comes along when other people put their trust in you for their careers and the financial support for their families," he says. "That's where I start in terms of looking at the role of leader and the responsibility that comes with that," Tim told me, going on to describe how he ignited change in the organization.

When Tim entered the job of U.S. chairman, he was confronted with a major issue involving past practices by the firm that required broad organizational change: "If you recognize a need to change and drive that change, it can be a much different process than when you fail to recognize a need to change and other people drive that change for you. One of the key things is to have the foresight to recognize a need to change and then have the will to drive that change, maybe even before others might see the need for that change."

But how do you capitalize on the opportunity and drive that change? Flynn says you must first have a compelling platform for change. Within KPMG, the people were willing to accept change. "That doesn't make it easy to change, but you have the receptivity to it," Flynn says. "Then you have to build the case for change—you have to communicate with everybody. You have to paint a picture. What does it look like on the other side of change?"

KPMG communicated through stories. The company created a series of 90-second videos in which people told their stories (for example, they'd been on a global assignment or done something else with great professional integrity). Then KPMG broadcast these videos. "[We] brought it to life so people could see what it meant to them," Flynn says. Then he and John Veihmeyer, the deputy chairman, talked to groups, always basing their discussions on their four priorities. "We created a whole new vocabulary around this," he says. "You have to have a consistent message; you have to keep saying it over and over and over again, until you're tired of saying it. Then people will finally get it. You can't veer off that message."

On December 8, 2007, KPMG broadcast live to 23,000 people through a satellite feed for two and a half hours. "It was all live; it wasn't scripted," Flynn recalls. "We just talked about our priorities. When you're going to drive a changed agenda, you have to have many different vehicles of communication—you have to have good personal communication and go through stories and illustrations, and you have to do it in your own words. You can't let other people write it for you."

Perhaps Flynn's messages are transmitted effectively because he so clearly loves his job; his openness is infectious. "I've got a fabulous job, right?" says Flynn. "I work with the smartest people. There's always a new challenge to tackle. Every day it's invigorating. All that being said, by the time something gets to my desk, it's either usually really good or really bad; there's not much in between. Top jobs aren't easy jobs, and I don't mean that in an egotistical way—they're very stressful. You do the best you can every day, you make the best decisions you can make every day, and there's a lot of fate that comes into play with these things as well. I can be dealing with stuff that happened five years ago but I had no involvement at all, and now I have to go deal with it. You probably get way too much credit when things go well and you get too much blame when things don't go too well. But to me, the most challenging and rewarding part is that you have the ability to impact a culture and you have the ability to drive change. And it's a very rewarding experience to be able to take an organization and improve its standing in the business community and to drive that process. It's an honor to be able to do that."

Wire-less

An interesting approach to communication comes from Richard Baker, CEO of Alliance Books. He admits to being "very selfish" in the communication medium he uses. He doesn't use email ("too slow and one-dimensional") or possess a BlackBerry. (A number of other leaders are strongly anti-BlackBerry: Says Monika Ribar of Panalpina, "I'm not a big email person. I don't have a BlackBerry. And I don't want to have a BlackBerry.")

Baker rarely writes a memo. Instead, he sends a lot of text messages (around 25 a day) and constantly talks to people. "If someone has a problem, he sends me a text, we talk, and the problem gets solved. I have lots of short telephone calls. Talking is a two-way dialog, so you learn much. If someone says it is urgent, I respond immediately. This is especially important in a newly merged company."

The day we spoke, Baker had begun the day by calling one of his store managers whose store had just broken a record. Imagine the motivational impact of having the CEO on the line. His second call had been to someone who had written to him with a few ideas after having read an article about the company. None of this is eye catching or headline making, but it is incredibly powerful in forging your own legend within the organization and in learning about what is really going on.

I haven't abandoned my BlackBerry, but I have learned how to use it to my advantage: I use it as an alarm, to keep an eye on what is going on. I respond only if it is something critical that needs my input quickly and directly, or if it requires arbitrating with a number of different parties to keep a process moving quickly. I have no compunction about switching off my BlackBerry on the weekend and when I am doing something else. I was once talking to an executive who told me about getting into bed one night with his BlackBerry; his wife turned to him and said, "Only one of us is staying in this bed tonight."

Face Time

One of the most striking examples of communication I have come across hails from Seung-Yu Kim of Korea's Hana Financial Group. His willingness to open communication channels with employees is deeply impressive. "My people can send me emails at any time, even very early in the morning, at two or three o'clock," he says. "They really appreciate it, and that's why they try to listen to me." At the company's training center, training finishes at nine or ten o'clock in the evening. Seung-Yu Kim makes a point of taking the opportunity to talk to the groups of 30 or 40 people. 'I talk with them personally and meet face-to-face with the people. And then I accompany them to one of the nearby small bars and drink Korean liquor, *soju*. Actually, I don't drink at all, so sometimes I drink water because the color is the same! It is about hugging them one by one.'

When any of Hana's people are hospitalized, Seung-Yu Kim always visits them in the hospital. The bank has 12,000 employees, so this is no mean feat. He also always attends the funerals of the parents of employees. "Our people are like my family," he explains. "If they have some trouble, they call me first."

The *E* in Communication

Whichever office I am in, I always walk around and talk to people. This is great for taking the pulse of a firm and measuring morale. Nothing really replaces face-to-face contact, even with the many other means of communication available, from videoconferencing to hand-written notes.

"I'm in a technology-rich environment," Patrick Swygert, president of Howard University, told me. "I don't know how many emails I get a day, but however many I get, I send out probably an equal number. Email and my BlackBerry are pretty much how I communicate today. The telephone is becoming more the exception than the rule.

On the campus [of Howard University], we have universal email, so you can send out a blast to all faculty, all students, all staff. It's so easy; but how many people actually read it is another matter."

Swygert knows the value of choosing the right words, be it in an email or a speech: "I took to heart a lesson that was given to me when I was an undergraduate. A professor told me that, in the best of worlds, you would speak to what you know with conviction, and you would speak to what you know with conviction in simple declaratory sentences. I've tried to do that my entire career—sometimes with success, sometimes not."

Jim Owens of Caterpillar echoes the thoughts of many I talked to. They were technologically savvy but wary of having their agenda hijacked by being available every single second of every minute of the day. "I don't allow myself to be the slave of email," Owens says. "My secretary screens them, and she gives me a priority call on things that I absolutely have to answer; if I don't answer them that day, she gets after me the next day. I never leave the phone on if I'm in meetings; I think it's rude to allow yourself to be interrupted in the middle of meetings. I don't carry my BlackBerry to meetings in the office. I use it extensively when I'm traveling, but never in the office. And I usually try, when I leave the office, between six and seven at night, not to do very much at home other than read the paper or magazine articles and things that are interesting."

In the age of the Internet, many senior executives offer their own weblog (blog) as a source of communication. Some leaders have found blogs to be a persuasive marketing tool; Jonathan Schwartz, CEO and president of tech giant Sun Microsystems; David Neeleman, founder and CEO of JetBlue Airways; and Richard Edelman, of Edelman, the largest independent PR firm in the world, are all avid corporate bloggers.

In his blog, Schwartz, says, "We've moved from the information age to the participation age, and trust is the currency of the participation age. Companies need to speak with one voice and be authentic.

Blogging allows you to speak out authentically on your own behalf, and in the long run, people will recognize that. Do it consistently, and they trust you."

Studies show that 45 percent of Fortune 1000 executives think that corporate blogs are growing in credibility as a way to develop and build brands. "For corporations, the attractions of corporate blogging are varied but include improving market status, personalizing customer relationships, boosting public relations, and improving recruitment," says Jose Esteves of Spain's Instituto de Empresa and an expert on corporate blogging. Corporate blogs are also being used to foster internal collaboration and improve knowledge management. "One of the key benefits of corporate blogging is that companies can track thousands of posts and know what Internet users are thinking about in real time," says Esteves. "For researchers, like me, it also offers a new mirror to see into the corporate soul."

What to Say

Jacques Aigrain, CEO of Swiss Re, offered a number of thought-provoking observations about communication. "It is quite a challenge to get some simple but motivating enough messages absorbed by the clerical staff, compared to the executive and management level," he says. "Especially if you're speaking about an esoteric risk business like ours, it can be horribly complicated in terms of the type of information you are dealing with to get the clerical staff to relate to what you are trying to do. Even in communication with the professionals, across various specialties, it is not that simple to create a crisp, simple enough message that everybody can put their hands on."

Leaders also must take into account the complexities of communication in a global business world. As Aigrain notes, most large companies involve a wide range of nationalities, who often speak English as their second language. In an ultrainternational organization, the home base might account for a tiny part of the real business, and the company might have a huge mix of nationalities at every level, from the board of directors on. If most of the organization is not speaking English as the native language, that creates a second communication challenge.

Another important communication issue that leaders point to is the need for effective education both internally and externally. How do you communicate a message that is sufficiently consistent for investors, stakeholders in the local community, the press, and internal personnel? "You cannot afford, in a public listed company, to have a significantly different communication internally and externally," says Aigrain. "You can have different nuances internally, but you cannot actually provide that much more data, as it becomes instantly disclosable. So you are considerably more limited now than you were 10 or 15 years ago."

Of course, companies must have totally different types of communication internally than externally. "It becomes a question of layering," says Aigrain. "[You have] one fundamental storyline, and then you peel off some more layers of the onions for the internal aspect, or you put some different emphasis or cast a different light for communication with the local community versus the investors."

The Communication Coda

But communicating what? The best leaders have an innate ability to identify what needs to be done today and what can wait. They know the key messages to communicate from day to day, from audience to audience. They prioritize constantly, aware that wars are lost by fighting on too many fronts. This requires great patience. "Everyone feels we're moving like a bullet," one leader confided, "but I feel like we're crawling." Pace is relative.

I have been surprised by how I can be misunderstood—and for me, it's not an English-language problem; it is a question of understanding, emphasis, and expression. I have modified how I speak, to make my vocabulary more simple and easy, in an attempt to get my message understood.

Each person reads material from his own perspective and takes his own meaning from what is written; you must try to predict that. This is true for both emails and the spoken word.

I recently had a conversation in an office about how resources would be allocated. The feedback two days later was that there would be no resources for those who were billing insufficient fees. This was not my message at all, but Chinese whispers are powerfully loud.

Similarly, I sent an email about a change in personnel to the whole firm. The message I got back from some quarters was that it was too harsh on the particular individual named. It was hard to explain that the individual in question had actually helped write the announcement.

The reality is that you want to do the right thing—to communicate and be clear and transparent. But you have to spend so much time making sure that the communication won't be misinterpreted or mis-understood by great sections of the organization that sometimes the timing isn't as swift as you'd like. And guess what? After all that, it still can get read the wrong way.

As a leader, if someone complains to you, you can't say, "Oh, yeah, right, I know what you mean—XYZ is a pain." You cannot jump on the bandwagon. And you need to decide whether you want to be one of the gang or whether you want to be a leader of the firm—you cannot be both. This is a difficult transition for most leaders.

I don't mind if people don't like me; that is human nature. But I want them to trust and respect me, and that takes time and is possible only with great communication, all the time. My own take on commu-nication is that it must follow a number of straightforward rules—ten, to be precise.

It Must Be Simple

"Whatever the message is, it is important to make it simple," says Carlos Ghosn, president and CEO of Nissan and president and CEO of Renault. "Complex messages are never understood. The only things that will be effective are things that are simple. Then people around you can understand and act on them." Renault and Nissan have three- to four-year business plans, with a maximum of three commitments that the company aims to achieve. This keeps the focus on those goals and enables limited and concrete milestones and objectives.

Complicated messages are harder to decipher. If you can say something simply, do so. This includes eradicating management-speak and jargon. The legendary U.S. investment guru Warren Buffett once opined that if he doesn't understand something, he assumes that someone is trying to fool him.

Plain speaking is not easy. Many organizations are steeped in a culture of management-speak. However, failure to communicate simply can be costly. In 1983, computer manufacturer Coleco wiped $35 million off its balance sheet in one quarter. The reason: Customers found the manuals for a new product line unreadable and swamped the company with product returns. In 1984, the firm went bust.

You also can never assume that your audience is on the same wavelength. I went to a friend's 40th birthday dinner in the United States. His daughter was asked to set the table. It was explained that the forks needed to be on the left and the knives placed on the right with their sharp sides pointed toward the plate. She got the forks right, but the knives were carefully placed at right angles to the plate. The girl had been helpful and had listened, but the final detail of communicating wasn't thought through. Imagine the room for misunderstanding in a global organization where there are—metaphorically, at least—knives and forks everywhere.

It Must Be Precise

Confusion is often the product of ambiguity. Don't say, "I want the project tomorrow." Specify what project, where you want it, and at what time. This gives much less margin for error. This way, if you actually want the project on your desk in the morning, you won't spend the day stressed out because the person delivering it thinks he has until midnight to email it to you.

Use Straight Talk from the Start

If you take over a company in a muddle—or worse—there is little to be said for politeness and understatement. Talk straight and act in accordance with what you say. Think of our earlier discussion about communication.

Face-to-Face Is Best—Even Now

In the information age, we have a huge choice of communication media: email, telephone, videoconferencing, and more. However, evidence suggests that none is as effective as good old face-to-face interaction. About 80 percent of human communication is nonverbal. Facial expressions, body language, eye contact—these are key conduits.

We read body language to pick up the atmosphere. We walk into a meeting and pick up the feel of what other people are thinking. We watch how Y reacts to what X is saying. You can't do that by videoconference. Body language speaks volumes. Ignore it at your peril.

"I believe a word from my mouth, or from anyone, has a strong soul," says Takeshi Niinami, CEO of Lawson in Japan. "If you talk directly instead of through email, and as long as you have a strong will, you can convey your will: 'This is right, let's get things done.'" In his early days in the job, Niinami estimates that he spent almost 70 percent of his time talking and listening to people face-to-face.

Niinami especially made use of team meetings. "You can have direct communication with 30 or 40 people rather than using email," he says. "Actually, I didn't use email at all—I just spoke on my own with the people." Niinami went to company training programs at Lawson University to talk to managers directly. For probably three months of the year, Niinami isn't in the office at all.

When I spoke to Monika Ribar, she had traveled the previous week from her office in Europe to Latin America. The sole purpose of the visit was the retirement party for a long-standing employee and manager who had been with the company for more than 30 years. 'The company sees that I am there, and this is very, very motivating for people," she says.

Make It Personal

Change and leadership begin with conversation. Bold decision making must always be backed by consistent and committed personal communication. "I sat down with probably 20 managers in the first week," says Stuart Rose, CEO of Marks & Spencer. "I said, 'Come in, sit down—you don't know me'—though one or two of them did remember me from my previous time with the company. I said, 'Tell me what you think the problems are in the business. Tell me what you think we should do, tell me how you think we should fix it.' There were those saying, 'I'm so glad that somebody like you has come in. You're talking about products, you're talking about prices, you're talking about shopkeeping. You know, if only we could do this, this, this, or this.' So you put them down as a tick."

Others were more stalwart: "There were others saying, 'There's no problem here; all you need to do is leave us to ourselves and go and do something else because my bit of the company is absolutely fine.' And there were those who weren't quite sure what to do. Interestingly enough, they were the most difficult ones because you had to make a very quick decision of whether you could get them there, or was it just going to take you too long? Can you teach this person to swim before the pool fills up, or can't you?"

Flatter management structures mean that executives can no longer rely on hierarchical power to get things done. Instead, managers must increasingly rely on persuasion—and inspiration. This requires a more sophisticated style of communication directed at the individual and imbued with emotional context as well as content.

One survey of 60 executives found that the messages that get attention are those in which the message is personalized, evokes an emotional response, comes from a trustworthy or respected sender, and is concise.

Great leaders have long been aware of this. Jack Welch of GE habitually wrote handwritten notes that he sent to workers at all levels, from part-time staff to senior executives. Some even framed his notes, as tangible proof of their leader's appreciation.

Seung-Yu Kim of Hana Financial Group told me about the amazing efforts he puts into establishing personal rapport with all the bank's employees. After Hana merged with several banks, Kim set out to memorize the names of many people as possible. He memorized almost a thousand.

"I had their photographs and their names, a CD in my car, and something on my desk, and even beside my bed," he says. "I tried to remember their names and their background, which province they came from, which school they graduated from. I tried to memorize them all. I also pop into branch offices whenever I can."

Be Yourself

Your communication style not only needs to be personal—it needs to be authentic, too.

"There is absolutely no chance of winning if you are not yourself," says Aigrain. "If you're not yourself, you stumble. Media training, to know their tricks? Absolutely. Basic communication experience? You learn on the job, too. But just be yourself because trying to be something else will create inconsistency between what you write and what you say, and how you say it."

Aigrain admits that he needed some time to get this aspect of his communication strategy right. Authenticity can cause problems at first, depending on your style; you have to see it through, though, and not change because of the initial reactions.

"First there was a feeling that I was maybe too brutal from the perspective of the community at Swiss Re, that I was the so-called 'bloody American banker type,'" Aigrain says. "Then phase two was, 'He may be a shark, but he seems to say things that may make sense.' Finally, once they saw the results, came phase three, which is, 'He has a big stick but he also means well and he cares, and he creates a dynamic and a momentum which we are ready to jump in.' But any variance in terms of the way I express myself or the tone that I used would have been interpreted inappropriately and perceived as a fake."

Watch the Context

It's not just what is said that matters, but the setting in which it is said. Talking to the boss in the bar or over lunch in the restaurant is a world away from a one-to-one in the boss's office. Often a power dynamic is involved in the choice of location. Be aware of it.

I was struck by the importance of knowing your audience when I spoke with Carl Schramm of the Kaufmann Foundation, the leading foundation in the United States for promoting entrepreneurship. Schramm is an author and actually says that he writes books for an audience of eight people (his board) and for the hundred people who work at the foundation. Beyond that, his work is picked up by many, many people, but he knows that the first two audiences are the ones that really matter. Every year, Schramm also writes a speech for the entire organization in which he maps out what the organization stands for and so forth. "This is partially symbolic," Schramm told me, "because a lot of people here are treasury clerks and so forth. They know

I'm out speaking to government ministers, politicians, and leaders. One of the implicit signals is, 'I stopped and wrote a speech for you because you're the people who count.'"

Regularity Breeds Contentment

"I've learned that people don't get the message until you hear it back from them," says Sesame Workshop's Gary Knell. "Once they start to repeat the message, then you know, okay, they're on the team."

Bruno Lafont, chairman and CEO of Lafarge, told me that he reads only direct emails but maintains constant communication in other ways. He meets with his executive committee team for three hours every week, and he meets with each of them individually once a month for one hour and when needed. Together, every month, they review the advancement on the group's few strategic and operational priorities. "We now have quarterly business reviews, and I attend many of them," Knell says. "I keep traveling a lot and try to meet informally as many local employees as possible, which ensures that I have a good understanding of what is going on in the business."

Leaders who are good communicators know it is essential to maintain a frequent dialog with their executive teams. It's no use hauling in an executive to give him a roasting if you haven't spoken to him for the previous month. Regular dialog should have removed the need for this. And remember that communication is a two-way activity. Key to this interaction is listening. "The best advice I was given is you've got to work hard at being a good listener—the higher you go, the more important that is," says Owens. "Most people who are highly successful are a bit of a bull in a china shop at some parts of their career. I had senior managers sit down with me, review my performance, and say, 'Here's an area that you ought to really work on.' I did try to take that to heart, and now I work very hard at creating a culture where people can feel very comfortable disagreeing with me. I want to engage in the fray and the debate. I want to get all their best ideas on the table— particularly from my direct-report team."

Monika Ribar, CEO of Panalpina, has a management team with five members and then has regional leaders all directly reporting to her. "Now, what is very important is that we cascade down the communication," she says. "It starts with communicating clearly, simply, and consistently. This is the most important thing. If you always tell people the same story, then if there is a change you need to announce it as a change.... This is so important."

Be Positive When You Can

You might feel tempted to slide into negativity. Any organization has a lot wrong with it—and that includes your own. No one you encounter is perfect—and neither are you. Accentuate the positive and use positive reinforcement to back your strategies. This was brought home to me talking to Niinami.

One of his strategies was to make the company's local branches receptive to local needs instead of being standardized by central dictate. "We are everywhere in Japan, and Japan has a very diverse culture and lifestyle," he says. "So we have to understand local customs and match up with local customs. We can't decentralize customer needs."

When the first stores started matching with local needs, the CEO was expected to issue a reprimand. Standardization had been the policy. Instead, Niinami praised the efforts of the stores in front of as many people as he could. "These kinds of things easily fly all over Japan," he says. "Some products—local products or local rated products—were failures. But I didn't give bad feedback. Basically, before I arrived, people didn't want to challenge the status quo—they just listened to management. They never thought on their own. I just pushed people to think on their own."

Negativity is corrosive. To stand any chance in the job, a leader has to quickly identify positive messages and continually emphasize them. Repetition of key messages is the hard graft of leadership.

Says Rose, "We tried, often via some very simple things, to give people their confidence back because the morale of the business was very damaged. There was a feeling of inevitability about the fact that we were a midmarket retailer either going to be undermined by cheaper competitors, like Matalan and Primark, or going to be completely swamped by competitors with mass appeal, like Tesco. We reminded people that this was not a new problem. We'd had competition through the preceding 110 years of our history in different forms and different shapes and different places. This was just another manifestation of the same problem, but this time we just weren't dealing with it." Rose reminded employees of the best things about Marks & Spencer: "*Quality, value, service, innovation,* and *trust* are the five words we always use, and the three most important things we need to do are to have better products, to have better shops, and to have better service," he says. "I still use those five words almost every day in this business, and I'm pretty certain now most people can remember them and say, 'Actually, he's got a point.'"

Communicate Up

Communication also needs to be channeled up the organization. This is an issue even for the CEO. The channel of communication between the CEO and the boardroom must be constantly open. In too many cases, CEOs seek to communicate with their boards when problems are mounting. On the other side, boards are often tempted to spring issues on unsuspecting CEOs at board meetings. Gamesmanship helps neither side win the game.

"I spend a lot of time communicating to the board," says Chip McClure of ArvinMeritor. "One of the things I put down as a key objective is to make sure that I meet with every individual board member at least once a year. I have one-on-one meetings with them, which means I fly wherever they are to have either lunch or dinner. I try to spend a couple of hours having face-to-face time with them."

Simpson Thacher & Bartlett chairman Dick Beattie says that he expects me, as a CEO, to provide strong leadership, to set a tone at the top that is unquestionably fair, ethical, transparent, and beyond reproach. "The CEO must also have considerable energy and unrestrained curiosity," Beattie says. "As chairman, I additionally expect the CEO to work closely with me in setting agendas, leading discussions and seeking help when needed." And he hopes the CEO would look to a nonexecutive chairman to get the most value from the board of directors and guide the board in providing oversight on the strategic direction of the firm.

The best CEOs spend time between the board meetings in touch with the board members, managing expectations, seeking advice, and taking soundings.

Clear and regular communication can turn around problems. One Fortune 100 company's fortunes had declined over ten years. By the time its board looked for help, it was, in effect, a turnaround. A new board with broader advisory skills took over, but within three years it became apparent that although the new CEO was effective at improving operations, he was not able to reposition the company's strategy. Eventually, another CEO was brought in. He created a weekly communication plan with the board to keep them abreast of the major strategic shifts and allowed an open forum in board meetings so that board members could witness the executive team in action. In this case, open and consistent communication helped the nimbleness of the company's decision making.

Key Points

- The core in the job description is communication.
- Communication must be constant; it must be simple, face-to-face as much as possible, personal rather than standardized, sensitive to context, and must move upward as well as downward.

Resources

Bains, Gurnek, et al. *Meaning Inc.* (London: Profile, 2007).

Brown, John Seely, Katalina Groh, Laurence Prusate, and Steve Denning. *Storytelling in Organizations* (Burlington, MA: Butterworth Heinemann, 2004).

Denning, Stephen. *A Leader's Guide to Storytelling* (San Francisco: John Wiley, 2005).

Steel, Jon. *Perfect Pitch* (New Jersey: John Wiley, 2006).

6

The Rise and Rise of the Global Leader

Increasingly, a leader's work takes place in a global arena. What does this really mean? If you're CMO of a tractor parts manufacturer in Deerpark, Ohio, what does the world matter?

"If I'm a 33- or 34-year old executive and I really want to do well, and my company has a global footprint, I've got to get out of Arlington, Virginia, at some point. I've got to be able to be flexible enough to do that and then, once landed in that otherwise alien environment, be open to its culture and language. You just can't stay put and be successful."

—*Patrick Swygert, president of Howard University*

Global Peoria

One of the most impressive global leaders I've encountered is Jim Owens, chairman and CEO of Caterpillar, Inc. Based in Peoria, Illinois, Caterpillar is one of those great unsung global success stories. With sales and revenues of $44.958 billion (in 2007), it is the world's leading manufacturer of construction and mining equipment, diesel and natural gas engines, and industrial gas turbines. There's nothing sexy about the industries in which it competes, but, like the company's leader, it is quietly and compellingly cosmopolitan. Much the same can be said of Peoria, the oldest settlement in Illinois. The town's

109

website is available in six languages. Perhaps there's an international gene in the water.

Owens joined the company in 1972 as a corporate economist. He worked in Geneva, Switzerland, in the 1970s. From 1980 to 1987, he was back in Peoria in the Accounting and Product Source Planning Departments. Then in 1987 he became managing director of Caterpillar's joint venture in Indonesia. He held that position until 1990, when he was elected a corporate vice president and ran a Caterpillar subsidiary in San Diego. In 1993, he came back to Peoria as vice president and chief financial officer. In 1995, Owens was named a group president and member of Caterpillar's executive office. Over the next eight years, as a group president, Owens was at various times responsible for 13 of the company's 25 divisions. In December 2003, the Caterpillar board named Owens vice chairman; he was appointed chairman and chief executive officer in 2004.

Owens says his international experience was vital to running a large multinational company. "It was invaluable for me to have lived and worked in Europe for five years. I lived in Indonesia for three years. I've traveled extensively in all the key countries. I understand how business happens there; I know a lot of people." Owens travels to Asia and Europe two or three times a year and Latin America once or twice a year. His senior executive group and most of the company officers also have lived and worked in other countries. "I think it's imperative to have a global perspective—to have lived and worked outside of your home country is an invaluable learning experience that no amount of travel will offset," he says. "[You learn] multiple things ... about how to work with a different government, with different business customers and dealers. You learn how to deal in a different language, you learn to be sensitive to cultural differences, tastes, preferences, and ways of doing things and ways of communicating."

Comings and Goings

Most successful fervent globalists have amassed international experience. Consider Rick Goings, chairman and CEO of Tupperware Brands, as well as chairman of Boys and Girls Clubs of America.

"We are global nomads," he says. "We don't really define ourselves by our nationality within the company. What's really good about this, I find, is that the culture we've developed in the company has transcended nationalism, and it's even transcended religion."

When Rick Goings came back to the States after being group vice president for Avon in Asia–Pacific, it was the first time in Avon's 100-year history that an executive had been sent overseas and came back to a more senior role. Previously, an overseas posting had been a highway to nowhere. "The worm has turned so much that we will not have a person in a senior role unless they've had that kind of experience," says Goings. "It isn't about taking a trip to Seoul or Hong Kong or Paris or Budapest. It's about living there—not just being sequestered in an expatriate community. That forever sensitizes us to listen and understand. It's almost like your whole approach to life changes."

Goings regards international experience as an alluring prospect for people on their route to a top job. It is part of the empowering experience of working for a global organization. "All corporations are today just loose collections of people, and the ones that can attract, develop, empower, and reward manage to retain those people," he says. "That's why I think today you've got to have leaders that are great communicators, who understand the importance of it, and also understand the importance of creating and operating a landscape that allows this empowered movement."

"You have to be a master at human potentiality development. Everyone is actually two people, the person they are today and the person they could become. When I first joined Tupperware, a senior

VP had to sign off before someone could have a phone installed! We have to keep finding ways of creating an environment in which people feel they can flourish—in essence to provide the soil in which they can grow. We find that they come for income, but really why they stay is the recognition and relationships. They feel that "here is a career path and this company cares about me." So we have found, and keep finding, more ways to recognize our people. This is all soft stuff, but I think soft stuff is the hard stuff when you are talking about loose collections of people."

Global Savvy

A lot of people like Jim Owens and Rick Goings have been shaped by their global business experiences. They are passionate believers that globalization is a good thing for both individuals and organizations.

Increasingly, research supports this view. Leaders say that globalization is making business more complex but is having a positive impact on their organizations, according to a PricewaterhouseCoopers survey of 1,410 leaders in 45 countries. Internally, the factors that led to increased business complexity for leaders largely included expanding their operations into new territories (65 percent), engaging in mergers or acquisitions (65 percent), and launching new products or services (58 percent). Externally, complexity was driven mostly by international, national, or industry-specific regulations, laws, standards, and reporting requirements, as well as by competitors' actions. Global growth is often centered on what Goldman Sachs has named the BRIC economies: Brazil, Russia, India, and China.

Global expansion presents several challenges for leaders to confront, including overregulation (64 percent), trade barriers/protectionism (63 percent), political instability (57 percent), and social issues (56 percent). But leaders view globalization in a positive light, with 58 percent saying it will have a positive impact on their firms in the next year and 63 percent seeing a positive impact in the next three years.

Look around the highest echelons of the corporate world, and, increasingly, you will see globalization at work. Leaders and senior executives are a more diverse group than ever, their backgrounds and careers impressively thick with global experiences. Times have changed. Back in the 1970s, an American executive was appointed to head the British coal industry. There was outrage at the very thought of such corporate carpet-bagging. Would the same debate occur today? I very much doubt it. British Airways has an Irish CEO following an Australian; Vodafone is led by Arun Sarin, an Indian-American; Americans Marjorie Scardino and Rose Marie Bravo run Pearson and Burberry, respectively.

Today global business is more than a political discussion point, marketing mantra, or corporate aspiration; it is a burgeoning day-to-day reality. One need only scan trade statistics to understand why.

More than half the S&P 500 companies now report revenues by geography. For them, international markets account for 33 percent of revenues, and their international business is growing nearly twice as fast as their U.S. business (9.1 percent annually versus 5.4 percent between 1998 and 2003). Not only is trade becoming more global, but the leading companies are as well.

The reality is that, as the business world has globalized, so has the executive job market, and the job of CEO in particular. Measures of corporate or personal success are now gauged in global terms. Increasing market share in home markets is unlikely to suffice as a measure of success.

Leaders are measured against global performance. Asked about key measures of his long-term success, Michael Critelli, then CEO (and now chairman) of Pitney Bowes, cites globalizing his company as a central benchmark. "We were a very insular U.S. company that exported to certain markets and was predominately strong in English-speaking markets," Critelli explains. "I am very excited that we are in many markets today where English is not the only language spoken. I want us to be confident and comfortable dealing across the globe."

An increasing cadre of globally savvy leaders is in Critelli's phrase, confident and comfortable wherever in the world they are doing business. Look at the names leading some of the world's biggest corporations. The world is their boardroom.

Coca-Cola is headed by E. Neville Isdell, a peripatetic Irishman who has worked for the company in Zambia, South Africa, Australia, the Philippines, and Germany. (I heard a story that when Isdell was working in eastern Europe, he fitted out a van with a table and eight seats and then drove around making stops to visit with salespeople, who climbed aboard the van to do their presentations.) The Alcoa CEO, Alain Belda, is a Brazilian citizen but was born in Morocco; Kellogg's CEO, Carlos Gutierrez, is Cuban; a Welshman runs L'Oréal; and the French Jean-Pierre Garnier heads GlaxoSmithKline.

Research by the Economist Intelligence Unit found that, of 250 companies in ten markets, the nationality of more than 18 percent of board members was different from that of the company they managed. This figure will certainly increase in the years to come.

The New Breed

None of this should come as a surprise. No significant company in the world can avoid competing globally or avoid global competition.

"Executive life has changed," says Laura Tyson, former dean of the London Business School, and former GE executive Nigel Andrews. (Andrews and Tyson led a research project into the emerging training requirements of organizations based on more than 100 face-to-face interviews with executives from global companies across a variety of industries and geographies.) "Only 20 years ago, the capabilities required of successful executives were functionally oriented. Apart from occasional forays to overseas subsidiaries, executive life was monocultural. The role of senior executives was carefully—perhaps comfortably—delineated. Communication was local and personal, and managed to fit the executive's convenience. Markets were monolithic and reassuringly stable."

Tyson and Andrews also point out that globalization does not simply involve the transfer of work to emerging economies: "Globalization is an art—an art of human relations which, like other arts, is premised on insights gleaned from teaching and from experience, and honed by continual practice, day in and day out, in the executive suites of the world's corporations. Globalization is about the exercise of management and leadership, on a worldwide scale."

As an exemplar of this new breed, consider Christopher Rodrigues, former CEO of Visa International, a business that recorded transactions of $4 trillion in 2006, thanks to its 1.2 billion cardholders.

Rodrigues is British, but his résumé is global, with education at Cambridge University and Harvard Business School, experience with McKinsey & Company, and senior positions with American Express, Thomas Cook, and Bradford & Bingley, which he led through its demutualization.

Global leaders such as Rodrigues offer a potent combination of skills and experiences. The box marked "Analysis" is ticked by Harvard and McKinsey. Then there is work with truly global organizations (American Express and Thomas Cook), as well as a leadership role at Bradford & Bingley. The foundations of this are general management skills. Rodrigues worked in advertising and marketing; his first job was selling dog food from the back of a car. Then he filled in the gaps in his knowledge of accounting at Harvard, where he added a broad range of basic skills and some sense of their interaction. The final element to this is diplomacy. When Rodrigues got the Visa job, his background reading was Margaret MacMillan's *Paris 1919,* which looks at the diplomatic machinations behind the creation of the League of Nations.

My view is that you will find it very difficult to be a global leader of any organization in the future unless you've experienced living in one or more regions. And companies that fail to give their individuals exposure to different cultures and a range of global experiences will lag behind.

Global Characteristics

But what are the characteristics and skills of these global leaders? If you wanted to create an identikit of the global leader, it would run something like this.

First, these leaders would possess experience in a number of global markets, as well as experience in marketing, operations, and finance. The résumé of Chris Rodrigues is no longer a rarity in its geographical and functional reach. In their book *Why Should Anyone Be Led By You?*, Rob Goffee and Gareth Jones point to the powerful influence of early experience in the sales function.

Experience is essential, but it must be interpreted and applied flexibly. Says Phil Hodgson, director of leadership programs at Ashridge Business School in England: "Older leaders need to work very hard not to let their decision making and their understanding of a situation be dominated by their past experience of success and failure. It is very hard to accept that what worked before may not—probably will not—work as well again. Equally, what failed last time does not necessarily define what will fail this time. The successful older leaders stay successful by reinventing themselves so that they employ the learning without deploying the methods gleaned from yesteryear."

The issue of age is also occupying the mind of Warren Bennis. Now in his late 70s, Bennis has gray hairs in abundance. Bennis is a leader. In World War II, he was the youngest infantry officer in the U.S. Army in Europe. "It shaped me so much and pulled from me things I may never have experienced," Bennis recalls. "I was very shy and felt that I was a boring human being, and then, in the course of being in the army, I felt that I was more interesting to myself. It was a coming of age, although I still didn't feel as though I was a leader."

For Bennis, the war was what he calls a "crucible"—"utterly transforming events or tests that individuals must pass through and make meaning from in order to learn, grow, and lead." The trouble for youthful leaders is that crucibles are rare and cannot be artificially reproduced. You can't re-create Nelson Mandela's Robben Island.

Bennis's book *Geeks and Geezers* (coauthored with Robert Thomas) examines a selection of "geeks," leaders between the ages of 21 and 35; and "geezers," men and women between the ages of 70 and 93. For many of the older leaders, the war and the Depression were crucibles in which their values were formed.

"The geezers were brought up in survival mode," Bennis explains. "Often they grew up in some poverty with limited financial aspirations. They thought that earning $10,000 a year would be enough. Compare that to the geeks, some of whom made a lot of money when they were young. They are operating out of a different context. If the geeks were broke, they would be more concerned with making a living than making history."

The message for would-be leaders is that leadership is founded on deeply felt experiences early in life. Youth might not be an obstacle to becoming a leader, but only if you have been through a crucible and emerged unscathed on the other side.

Culture Clubs

A second element crucial to the global leader relates to culture. Nowhere is the ability to act efficiently and innovatively in an unpredictable business environment more vital than in the C-suite. Global leaders need to be comfortable with people from a range of cultures. Business leaders must keep in mind that country-specific cultures are still important.

Examples abound of business leaders who have tried to impose their way of doing things and have encountered culture-based resistance. It is still happening. Recently, an American executive was appointed to run a bank in Asia. He got there and told everyone that what they were doing was basically wrong, not the way it needed to be done. He lasted six months because, although he could run a U.S.-based global bank, an Asia-based global bank offered an entirely different set of cultural challenges.

It is worth remembering that different ways of doing things offer different opportunities, both business and personal ones. The Indian electrical equipment company Anchor came up with a vegetarian toothpaste. Most varieties actually use a small amount of meat product in some way. For vegetarian Indians, this was a definite nonstarter. Anchor created a new niche in the market.

Being a global leader requires a certain cultural sensitivity, as many have told me. "Cultural awareness is important—being reasonably sensitive and aware of the differences and nuances between America and Europe, between the different countries in Europe and between Asia and the rest of the world," says Jacques Aigrain, CEO of Swiss RE. "So being a global CEO is about cultural awareness—making people understand it is one single company, one pool of capital, one single duty to the shareholder, and so not being particularly flexible with regard to local compromises."

Although leaders must tread carefully in different cultures, they also must champion the company's global needs. Not bowing to the demands of the local business at the expense of the global business is particularly important, emphasizes Aigrain. "There are plenty of local rules and regulations, but there's absolutely no reason why the culture you create for the firm, and the way you want to do business, should be compromised by the perceived local circumstances. You want one standard, and from our perspective, you want to apply it in the same form everywhere. You don't want a local management which gets overly influenced by a local view rather than the global interests of the firm."

I realized early on when I came to Europe that my leadership approach would need to change. Americans and, to some extent, Asian countries generally enjoy a far more directive management approach. They expect the leader to lead. In Europe, I could not dictate and direct what I wanted to do (if I wanted anyone to actually do it). Instead, I needed to consult and then discuss and listen to the thoughts of others. Even if I didn't use the suggestions given to me, the Europeans needed to be consulted. This meant decisions took longer to make, but in the long run, it was worth it because I gained the trust and loyalty of my European colleagues.

Staying Power

A third element is sheer staying power. The skills required of global leaders are demanding. So is their schedule. Witness the travel plans of WPP CEO Sir Martin Sorrell: Over the course of the year, he goes to one major region. In 2007, he went to Latin America for two two-week trips. In alternate years, he goes to Asia. Asia and Latin America account for about 25 percent of the company's business, so this trip is increasing in importance. He also goes to New York once or twice a month, usually for a week at a time. In addition, he frequently schedules one-, two-, or three-day trips to Europe.

Such schedules are not unusual. Indeed, if you run a global organization, they are expected. Physically and mentally, such levels of travel are demanding. (More on that later.)

The Talent Market

The number of accomplished and energetic global leaders will undoubtedly continue to rise as the pace of globalization intensifies. Demand for global leaders will grow. In India, for example, as companies expand, they increasingly need business leaders who have broader international experience. Local managers can utilize plentiful Indian manpower, but very different skills are needed to launch products and brands in foreign markets.

This poses fundamental questions about how we prepare executives for leadership roles in global organizations. Indeed, some doubt whether ease with global business can be acquired. Gary Knell, CEO of Sesame Workshop, has worked extensively throughout the world. He worked in Asia at the time of the widespread economic collapse and the handover of Hong Kong. "It was a tumultuous time in business and economics. The baht was devalued overnight, the parent company I was working for had a lot of financial challenges, and I was trying to manage the publishing piece of that company and we were cash-strapped," Knell recalls. "I was under fire. I had to make decisions about who would be on the payroll one day and who would not be, and what bills we needed to pay on Friday or put off to the following week."

Knell says that experience tested his executive decision making. "Everything since that time almost pales in comparison with the pressure that I was under," he says. Knell also gained valuable skills from operating between cultures. "I had a staff made up of virtually every ethnic group in the world. I loved that. I loved being around that kind of diversity."

Knell does not underestimate how hard it is to be a truly global leader: "It's like it's genetic, and it's really hard to teach someone how to work effectively on a global basis if they don't have it in their own blood. I think having a global perspective is something that really you have in your blood, and it's not for everybody. There was an advertising campaign which asked, 'Is your company truly global, or are you just all over the place?' I always remember that because you can be all over the place or you can really have a global perspective. I try to surround myself with people who can understand a global perspective and go between cultures."

Another leader with formative global experience is Chip McClure of ArvinMeritor. McClure lived in Germany from 1992 to 1995 and says he didn't really understand what it meant to be a global person until then. "I had traveled extensively before that. I had spent a lot of time in Japan. I was responsible for many of our overseas joint ventures. But if I was honest about it, I would get on a plane, fly business class, go stay in a business hotel, be there Monday to Friday, and then fly back home," he told me. "It wasn't until a Sunday morning in the middle of winter that I had to call and try to communicate in German, to convince a plumber to come out and fix the heating system because the family was sitting there freezing, that I really realized what being a global person was."

As Knell and McClure's comments suggest, the identikit global leader I described is not the product of a two-year MBA program, but the culmination of decades of development and experience in truly global settings. Such global *savoir faire* is not easily acquired. Given that fewer than 25 percent of Americans have a passport, the number of potential global leaders likely to emerge from the United States is more limited than you might think. "Very few American managers really can think global," says Monika Ribar of Panalpina. "In Europe, we are multicultural—always have been."

Nor is the global leader necessarily provided by the world's business schools. At Harvard Business School, non-Americans are 33 percent of the MBA intake. At the University of California's Anderson School, the figure is 24 percent. There's a long way to go if the undoubted future demand for global leaders is ever to be met.

So let's take a look at what companies on the global front line need to do.

Take Regular Soundings

Companies must create systems and networks that allow them to key into the major global trends. Lafarge has an international advisory board that helps alert the company to geopolitical and international trends. "This is invaluable," says Bruno Lafont, Lafarge's chairman and CEO. "It gives us the opportunity to benefit from the experience of key international economic leaders. They contribute to the molding of the group's prospective international vision." The board meets twice a year for a two-day session. One meeting is held in France and covers some of the biggest issues of the modern world, such as environmental management, research, and cultural dialog. The second meeting focuses on further understanding the development of a country or a region; the two last trips were dedicated to South Africa and China. Board members listen to leaders on the political, economical, and social aspects of the country. Industrial groups based in the country comment on the conditions in which they develop their business. Lafarge then gains the benefit of their experience and gets a deeper understanding of geopolitical and economic trends.

Acquire the Talent

With deep and deepening pockets, some emergent companies can now buy the talent they need. Lenovo's acquisition of the PC business from IBM Consulting, for example, allowed Lenovo to absorb a cadre of globally trained managers into its organization. This is an option for companies with deep pockets, but assimilating people after an acquisition is notoriously difficult.

Invest in Developing Experience

"We have to develop people who can understand globally and locally," says Takeshi Niinami, CEO of Lawson. Companies in both emerging and established economies need to invest in the middle ranks of executives to give them the necessary global experience to succeed in the future. Sending senior executives around the world is good, but it is not enough. Executives must be sent at a much earlier age to learn languages and understand different cultures. Immersion is more useful than accumulation of air miles.

Hire Indian and Asian Talent

The onus is also on Western companies to hire talent from Asia. They need to introduce high-potential Asian executives into their systems early enough to inculcate them with their cultures and competences. They need to develop the management talent of the future. Most organizations don't do this; they look in local markets only when they have to. This is a talent Band-Aid.

Get on the Road

I heard a story about a Korean CEO who was interested in an opportunity in Bangladesh. When he arrived in Bangladesh to meet the minister of telecommunications and to visit some potential sites, he got in a car from the airport. The car made it a few yards before it was stoned by passersby. There was a strike, and no cars were allowed to be on the road. The CEO was undeterred. He eventually hired an ambulance for the day. Even during a strike, no one stones an ambulance.

The travel itineraries of global executives are daunting. But there is no substitute for being there long enough to see and understand what's really happening. Too often, executives fly in, meet and greet local executives, and reboard the plane. They spend too much time traveling and not enough time looking, listening, talking, and seeing local market realities with their own eyes. One retail chain opened a store in an Asian market in completely the wrong location. Why? When the team made a flying visit to locations, it was the rainy season and the roads were all washed out. Because they couldn't see where the roads were, they made a costly mistake based on inaccurate local information. That isn't a mistake a truly global leader would make.

"I change the people rather than change their minds—it takes too long time to change their minds," says Seung-Yu Kim of Hana Financial Group. "So I now wait about six months or one year. If I notice they're not going to change their mind, I change the people. That's why I try to find the right person. That's a key job for me: to find the right person." Hana now recruits from China and also sends about 10 to 15 people to China every year to learn the Chinese language. Kim says then they can start to try to understand the Chinese culture and the people's minds. About a hundred employees can speak Chinese, and Hana has five branch offices in China. They've also tapped into the nearly one million Koreans living in southern California, especially in the Los Angeles area, by working with one of the investment banks to take over one of the Korean community banks over there. Of course, Hana must tweak its approach a bit. "Even though they're Korean and can speak Korean, their culture is different from pure Koreans, so we need to understand the Korean-American culture," Kim says. "We're sending our people to southern California to understand what they think about Korea and what they think about America."

Key Points

- Globalization is a business reality for every person in a top job—or should be.

- Globally savvy leaders have broad-ranging functional and international experience that they apply flexibly and appropriately. Their experience is not enshrined in stone, but open to new interpretations.

- In addition, they are sensitive to different cultures and the cultural nuances of different situations. They have the stamina necessary for global travel.

- The rise of the global leader provides four challenges for organizations. (1) They must ensure that they acquire truly global executives. (2) They must invest in their development; global skills require global development. (3) They must, in particular, hire talent from the burgeoning Asian and Chinese economies. (4) They must encourage their people to get on the road.

Resources

Andrews, Nigel. "Global Business Capabilities." *Business Strategy Review* 15 (Summer 2004): 4–10.

Bennis, Warren, and Robert Thomas. *Geeks and Geezers* (Boston: Harvard Business School Press, 2002).

Crainer, Stuart. "Christopher Rodrigues: Visa, Vision, and Verification." *Business Strategy Review* 17.2 (Summer 2006): 23–25.

Goffee, Rob, and Gareth Jones. *Why Should Anyone Be Led By You?* (Boston: Harvard Business School Press, 2006).

PricewaterhouseCoopers. *9th Annual Global CEO Survey*, 2006.

Tyson, Laura, and Nigel Andrews. "The Upwardly Global MBA." *Strategy+Business* 36 (Fall 2004): 60–69.

7

Me, Myself, and I

You're under pressure from all sides—investors, your boss, your board, not to mention your people, unions, competitors ... and more. How can you keep your sanity and live happily when you could (should?) be working and traveling 24/7? One answer is how well you are networked internally and externally. This becomes a bigger issue the bigger the job is. If you want to beat the risk of isolation, you need a web of contacts, colleagues, and mentors to talk to and turn to when the going gets demanding.

> "We demand a lot from our top people, more now than perhaps at any other point in the last century. Forget about 9 to 5, or 7 to 7, or 6 till 10. The cell phone, Internet, and Black-Berry changed all that. Now we can work 24 hours a day, across every region in the world. Ever spent an afternoon at the in-laws' quietly closing a deal? I have. Ever gone on vacation and thought, 'Just a little peek at my email won't hurt?'"
>
> —*A CEO*

Chief Network Officer

Being a leader involves a central paradox: It is the most notable and eye-catching role, but it can also be the loneliest. As a leader, you get the attention, the welcome at the airport, and the welcoming committee when you visit an office. Then you're sitting in a taxi on the way back to the airport, and you know your name will go against the decision.

One of the biggest threats to anyone in a top job is isolation. A leader is often in a new industry with a new team. And everyone expects instant results. The potential for isolation is enormous. Being aware of this is crucially important.

"I didn't appreciate the problem of isolation," Richard Baker of Alliance Boots told me. "I needed a private advisory group of people I could talk to who would empathize and understand the issues I was dealing with. There are times when it is very complex and you really don't know what to do, so I built up this network of people. I talk to a businessman coach outside the company and, in particular, my father. You really need someone else to talk to."

Ironically, perhaps the loneliest job in the world belongs to a CEO who is brought in when the company founder is still *in situ* as chairman. Think of Phil Knight at Nike, who brought in William Perez as CEO. Perez lasted a mere 13 months. At Apple Computer in the 1980s, Steve Jobs recruited John Sculley to take the company on to the next level with his marketing experience at Pepsi. It didn't last. Founders like Ted Waitt of Gateway, Michael Dell, and Charles Schwab have failed to resist the temptation to return as CEOs. There are many other examples of unpassed torches.

Whether they have a founding father looking over their shoulder or not, you must invest time in building relationships with key influencers both inside and outside the organization. This might be only a handful of people, but they are the people whose views count in the organization and whose views can make or break a leader's tenure.

Responses differ. Some leaders bring in someone they can trust to share the burden. Others take a different route. When he took over as CEO of Ocean DHL, John Allen eschewed the option of bringing outsiders straight into the management team. He wanted to show that he thought the people in the organization were up to the job and to give them an opportunity to shine. This was a statement of faith, but not of blind faith. Later he recruited an external CFO and COO.

So being a leader can feel lonely. But the good news is that the feeling is something of an illusion. When you start thinking about it, you quickly realize that you have a huge network of family, friends, and colleagues who you can call upon and who want you to succeed.

Caterpillar's Jim Owens agrees: "Running a megacompany, like Caterpillar, is about having a great leadership team, great cohesion, and understanding of the business and industry so you can lay out the broad strategic direction, stake out very bold goals for what you hope to achieve, and then work with a great team of people who really understand all aspects of the business and cascade that down to a work agenda for the whole organization." Owens also points out the necessity of having support on the home front. "It'd be very difficult to have this job and not have a wife who was a partner—my wife is just great support," he says. "We've moved the family around the world—Geneva, Switzerland, Djakarta, Indonesia, Nassau, San Diego, back and forth to Peoria. She does that with full recognition of everything I've got to do and the fact that she's got to do a lot of things with me, if we're going to stay together as a team."

The Odd Couple

At the very top, the relationship between the CEO and the chairman is key. "I have a very close exchange with my chairman," says Monika Ribar of Panalpina. "I try to talk to him, certainly at least once a week or even twice a week, to inform him, to talk to him, to also get his feedback."

With boards becoming more independent and the chairman's role being split from the CEO, the relationship of the CEO, chairman, and board of directors will be increasingly crucial to how a company performs.

Historically, the CEO and chairman roles have often been combined in American corporations. Now separation is common, thanks to corporate governance guidelines that require greater distance between the board and the CEO, to encourage objectivity.

A study by the governance ratings firm GovernanceMetrics International (GMI) found that 95 percent of the FTSE 350 firms rated by GMI split the roles of CEO and chairman. In France, where the combined CEO/chairman has traditionally been a powerful force, more companies are moving in this direction, with companies such as Renault and Carrefour splitting the roles. In Germany, the roles of the chairman as head of the supervisory board and of the CEO as head of the management board are separated in law.

More companies are splitting the chairman and CEO positions. A survey by Institutional Shareholder Services of 1,433 companies that make up the various Standard & Poor's indexes, including the S&P 500, found that 41 percent had separate chairmen and CEO positions in 2006, up from 37 percent in 2005.

Among the higher-profile companies to split the jobs in 2006 was troubled Ford, where chairman Bill Ford, Jr., gave up the CEO post to newcomer Alan Mulally, who moved to the troubled car maker from Boeing.

Also notable, some high-profile CEOs have become chairmen of major corporations. This suggests that they see the roles as powerful rather than ambassadorial—examples include former Nokia CEO Jorma Ollia becoming chairman of Shell, and AstraZeneca recruiting Louis Schweitzer, the ex-Renault boss, as its chairman.

When it comes to healthy CEO/chairman relationships, best practice is rarely reported. Agreement between CEOs and chairmen is not a great media story. A wide range of approaches is used. Some chairmen are hands-on, whereas others have a light touch. No formula exists. Successful instances often involve founders moving from the CEO's job to become chairman. Consider Microsoft chairman and

CEO Bill Gates handing over the CEO reins to long-time colleague Steve Ballmer in 2000; eBay company founder Pierre Omidyar becoming nonexecutive chairman with Meg Whitman as CEO; and Intel's Andy Grove becoming chairman, with Craig Barrett as CEO.

There are other instances of a CEO and chairman working together to turn around an ailing company, or the chair acting as a supporter to help a new CEO make the transition into the role. But it is a complicated relationship. The chairman can essentially fire the CEO. "You can have only a *professional* relationship with your chairman," one CEO told me.

Think Team, Not Board

In reality, the most effective boards are high-performance teams. As with all effective teams, members have clearly defined roles, play to their strengths, and complement each other. CEOs need to think of boards as part of their team instead of a sometimes irritating supervisory body.

Looking at boards in this way offers a different and potentially important perspective. Jeffrey Sonnenfeld, senior associate dean for executive programs at the Yale School of Management, and a corporate governance expert, has observed, "We need to consider not only how we structure the work of a board, but also how we manage the social system a board actually is. We'll be fighting the wrong war if we simply tighten procedural rules for boards and ignore their more pressing need: to be strong, high-functioning workgroups whose members trust and challenge one another and engage directly with senior managers on critical issues facing corporations."

A similar perspective comes from boardroom expert Edward Lawler: "A board is a group—perhaps, in some cases, a team. Boards need to be assessed by the same conditions and behaviors that lead groups to be effective."

I see the board as a vital network. "I've heard it said that the board provides the cheapest advice the CEO will ever get. I've been a consultant for a large part of my career, and, as a board member, the company and CEO have free access to me," says Jill Kanin-Lovers. "That's why who you put on your board also is very important." Kanin-Lovers says it's not uncommon for the new CEO to look at the board and say, "Hey, I could use maybe some counsel in this area and I don't see it reflected on this board" or "You know, maybe there are folks on this board who I don't think are giving me fresh thinking." She points out that the board's job is to move beyond providing oversight and to serve as a resource to the CEO. Thus, the board must have the right composition to reflect that.

There's Always More to Give

You realize pretty soon that you need support from every network you can lay your hands on. As a leader, it didn't take long to realize that it is a very different job from any other position. For me, it seemed straightforward. It was "just" a promotion. My employer didn't change. I grew up in Heidrick & Struggles and have friends and colleagues whom I have worked and played with for years. Suddenly, though, when I became CEO, people stood outside my office talking but wouldn't come in.

That wasn't the only change. My days were longer and busier than ever. Although I was based in London at the time, I needed to be visible to all our offices across the world. I traveled constantly. The impression the leader portrays tells people how the company is doing; I needed to be up, positive, and engaged all the time. And I still do.

Inevitably, it takes a toll on home life. I'm on the phone one minute talking to my CFO; the next I'm arriving home to be greeted by my 8-year-old daughter, and the first thing she asks is, "Dad, do you know where my Nintendo DS is?" I routinely eat dinner standing up in the kitchen because everyone else has eaten already and I have only an hour and a half before the next conference call. When my son's tooth fell out, the "tooth fairy" had only euros and pounds in his pocket—not much good for a little boy expecting a couple dollars under his pillow.

One night, I read my 4-year-old son a bedtime story, and he asked, "Daddy, are you traveling this week?"

"Only to Germany for one day," I replied. "I'll be back in time to read you a story."

"Dad, where is Germany? Is that near the grocery store?"

Actually, I have found that I don't talk about work at home—I almost don't want to relive it all again. It's a challenge because I'm dealing with work issues all day, from early morning until I get home at 8 PM or later. And I want to switch off. I don't want to relive anything; I want to sit and unwind and relax in my comfort zone. It was tougher when my children were younger because I'd walk in the door and my wife would hand me a baby. "Can I just get five minutes to take off my suit first?" I'd ask.

Like many people in a top job, I inhabit two separate worlds, with everyone demanding my time and attention. Sometimes I worry whether I have enough to give. One day I read a book called *The Giving Tree* by Shel Silverstein to my youngest son. It's a story about a tree and a little boy.

Every day the boy comes to swing on the tree's branches, to eat its apples and sleep in its shade. The boy loves the tree. And the tree loves the boy. But as the years pass, the boy finds other things to do and the tree is often alone.

After much time has passed, the boy comes to the tree and asks for money. The tree suggests he pick its apples and sell them in the city. This makes the boy happy; he picks all the apples and goes away. And he stays away for a long time.

One day the boy comes back—he wants to build himself a house. The tree suggests he cut off its branches. This makes the boy happy; he cuts off all the tree's branches and goes away to build his house.

He stays away for a long time and is old when he returns. He is unhappy and fed up with life, and wants a boat so that he can sail far away. The tree tells him to saw its trunk in two and make a boat. This makes the boy happy; he hollows the tree's trunk into a boat and sails away.

The tree (now a tree stump) is alone. After many years, the boy comes back; he is now very old and sad. And the tree is sad, too, because he feels he has nothing left to give the boy.

The boy tells the tree that he is just so very tired and needs to sit down. The tree suggests that the boy sit on his stump and rest. And the boy does, and the tree is happy; it was wrong when it thought it had no more to give the boy.

Being a leader can feel like being a giving tree. At work—and at home—people need you to give more. I am learning to embrace and understand this, and to view it as a privilege rather than a hardship.

Hard at Work

I am not alone. There may be giving trees, but there are also unforgiving trees. I was talking with Richard Baker when he was CEO of Alliance Boots, and he told me a story about how he broke his shoulder when he fell out of a tree because he was just trying to be a good dad. His daughter wanted to climb a tree, but he was tired from jet lag and working away all week, so he wasn't really concentrating as he climbed. He missed his step and fell to the ground. Tired leaders and trees don't mix.

All the leaders I have talked to over the years reveal much the same trouble with balancing hectic schedules and family life. The family is the ultimate supportive network. "I take my family vacations, I spend time with my kids and wife and carve it out. But, you know, you've got to work about as hard at that as you do your job," says Owens.

This was also an issue that Jim Skinner of McDonald's tackled. "You know, we all work hard. I've seen a lot of people work hard, and they confuse effort with results; that's a danger. I think that's sort of dumbing down the whole concept around hard work. I'd rather say, 'Let's work smart.' It makes more sense."

I asked Ribar how she spends her time. Her reply was typical. "I constantly exchange information with my people. I'm looking at putting the right people in the right places. I meet with people, some of whom I want to hire. Then, of course, when I travel, companies give me presentations and we have discussions. Certainly, the biggest part of my time, in the office or also when I'm traveling, is spent talking to people. And then there is preparing for meetings, especially executive board meetings or actual board meetings. Finally, there are all the presentations I give. At the moment, everybody wants me for a speech—there are not that many women leaders."

Says Peter Sharpe, president and CEO of Cadillac Fairview Corporation, "I've always worked a lot and long hours, but I rarely ever bring work home. I've always been able to close the door of the office and make that break. I love what I do and I enjoy time with my family, but you sacrifice a lot if you aspire to grow and run an organization. There's lots of sacrifices along the way."

One of the striking features of globalization is that it is creating a 24/7/365 business culture. Depending on your point of view, this is either a good thing or a bad thing. But it is also making the job of the CEO a 24/7/365 watch.

Overwork is not good for CEO health. Nor is it good for business. In the United States, a National Sleep Foundation study found that people who work more than 60 hours a week make almost 10 percent more mistakes on the job than people who work less.

For many leaders, burning the corporate candle at both ends and in the middle is a fact of life. A report at the 1999 Davos World Economic Forum put it succinctly: "Leaders are increasingly suffering from stress, sleep deprivation, heart disease, loneliness, failed marriages, and depression, among other problems. And those woes are taking a toll on the bottom line. Leaders must avoid workaholism. No matter how much they enjoy their jobs, they must avoid overworking when it renders their home life so unpleasant that the office becomes happier than the home."

It's hard to argue with such sentiments, but the reality is often stark. One survey found that nearly one in two leaders in Canada placed their firms ahead of their families in importance. The number who would not cut short a business meeting to celebrate their wedding anniversary was also nearly one in two.

There's one person whose emails I always read: my wife's. I remember one particular email, which I received on my BlackBerry just as I touched down in Hong Kong for a three-week trip to Asia. The email was empty, but the subject line read, "You forgot to change the light bulbs." It was the one thing she had asked me to do before I left.

I was thinking my next book would be called *Husband or Wife of a CEO*. During the research for this book, the incredible patience of the CEO spouse has come up again and again. Leaders nearly always mention their home life and the insight and support they couldn't do without.

"I see two types of leaders: Some of them are obsessed by their businesses, and it is really a lot of their life; and there's another group who see it as a big part of their life, but their family is important to them, and they need a life for themselves. And, a lot of those leaders are supported by long-term family relationships, and families, and they seem to be more focused on looking after their watch, and then building a legacy," says Steve Tappin, partner in the CEO/Board practice of Heidrick & Struggles. "The relentless leaders keep going until the company is number one and is perceived as number one. For the others, if they've taken the company forward and they've looked after all the stakeholders, the company has been successful. These are the more balanced leaders."

Balancing the Week

Definitely in the balanced category is Chip McClure of ArvinMeritor. I asked him about his schedule. "I tend to get in early. I think the only person that gets in before me in the morning is my CFO. I'm usually in by 6:30; he's in by 6:00, so he's got the coffee made, which is nice," he told me. "There is no average week. If I look at my calendar for a full year, there's obviously certain things which are locked in, starting with board meetings, committee meetings, various shareholder meetings, analyst meetings, earnings calls, that type of thing. So within each week there may be those kind of things interspersed."

Consider McClure's schedule for the upcoming week when he talked to me: "If I look at next week, on Monday, I'm meeting with one of our heavy truck customers; on Tuesday and Wednesday, I'm going to be in Washington, D.C. One of the things I try to do is spend time in Washington not only as a representative for the company, but also to represent the automotive industry. So I've got a number of [Capitol] Hill visits with Senators and Congress people. Then on Thursday I'm visiting with a company that's totally outside of our industry, just to do some benchmarking on technology. The company I'm meeting with has done a tremendous job reinventing itself by developing innovative technology. Then the following week, I'll be visiting some of our global facilities. Two weeks ago, I was in Mexico and visited six or seven of our plants. Obviously, I spent the majority of my time with our people, but at a few of the facilities, I also took the time to meet with some of the local elected officials."

McClure is famed for his ability to ensure that meetings run on time. "The only thing you can't recapture is time," he says. He has three strategically placed clocks in his office. "These clocks are in place because I don't normally like meetings to last more than an hour. I understand that sometimes a meeting might have to go a little longer because of the content, but when we hit 45 minutes and haven't gotten through all of the items, I'll say, 'Listen, we've got 15 minutes left—what do we need to get resolved? Let's get it resolved, and let's move on.' Because there's only 24 hours in a day."

Present and Incorrect

The problem with their unrelenting schedules is that leaders set the pattern for everyone in the organization. Executives quickly learn to imitate the style of the person at the top. If that person is a workaholic (as virtually all leaders are), it is hardly surprising that the cult of presenteeism continues. American leaders tend to be among the worst offenders. "Americans have more money because they have less leisure," MIT's Lester Thurow has simply noted.

This is not just an American thing. A five-year tracking study by Les Worrall and Cary Cooper for the U.K.'s Institute of Management and the University of Manchester Institute of Science and Technology found that the work and home life balance was still a pipe dream. More than 80 percent of executives worked over 40 hours a week, and one in ten worked over 60 hours. A resounding, though depressing 86 percent said that the long hours had an effect on their relationship with their children, and 71 percent said that it damaged their health.

"We want to have it all. More money—and more time. More success—a more satisfying family life. More creature comforts—and more sanity. We can work hard, we can find love and have a family, and we can enjoy the fruits of our success," concludes a survey by *Fast Company* magazine and Roper Starch Worldwide. It is a sobering thought that several disasters over the past 20 years involved employee sleep deprivation, including Chernobyl, the *Challenger* explosion, and the *Exxon Valdez* oil spill.

Many of today's leaders could learn a lesson from another famous business leader of the past: John D. Rockefeller, president of Standard Oil. During his lifetime, Rockefeller came under much criticism, as well as some odd mythologizing. A persistent story focused on his phenomenal capacity for hard work and long hours, a trait Rockefeller strenuously denied.

"People persist in thinking that I was a tremendous worker, always at it, early and late, winter and summer," said Rockefeller. "The real truth is that I was what would now be called a 'slacker' after I reached my middle 30s....I never, from the time I first entered an office, let business engross all my time and attention."

Rockefeller lived to the ripe old age of 97.

On the Road

Energy is undoubtedly a prerequisite for the job. Leaders also expect it of the people they work with. "One of the things I look for most in people is energy levels," Robert Devereux, former CEO of Virgin Group, observed. "I won't employ people who don't have high energy levels because they won't last. People with energy—they're self-motivated, they get going, they get things done."

Yes, you need energy to be in a top job, and the more you have, the better. Energy levels are most obviously tested by the vast amounts of travel that come as part of the job. "I travel a great deal," one COO told me. "My home office is in a suburb of Washington, D.C., but I spend a great deal of my time on the road—in excess of 50 percent. So I am in the office less than half the time."

That's pretty typical. The reality as a twenty-first-century leader is that you are on the road most of the week. You do overnight flights because you're commuting, and when you get to the weekend, you're tired, and perhaps not as patient as you should be. Says Owens, "I don't know how you can be a CEO and not know how to sleep on an airplane. I sleep about as well overnight to Europe as I do at home in bed."

I recently had breakfast with an Asian business leader. I said, "So you flew in last night—how was your dinner?" He said, "I had the standard dinner, from the mini bar—scotch and some peanuts." I laughed because I know how accurate that is.

Personally, I don't mind the flying because that's a great time to catch up on reading articles, books, client information, and magazines. Every leader I know reads a lot—and all the time—and they all say they need more time to read. But who doesn't?

Having said that, the jet lag can be really tough. Like anyone else, I sometimes struggle in the afternoon: It's not like you become superhuman when you take on a top job; it still hits you. I don't sleep well—but I think most leaders would say the same, and most people I know in leadership keep a notebook by their bed to remember all those thoughts that come to them as they lie awake in the middle of the night. And most would also agree that when they write down that one thought and switch off the lamp, they think of another five they want to write down.

Roads Well Traveled

It's worth remembering that today's traveling business leaders follow in a long tradition. From the earliest times, trade has relied on the willingness of individuals to suffer personal privation and hardship to transport themselves and their merchandise to their customers. One of the most celebrated Western business travelers was Marco Polo, who chronicled his travels in China, accompanying his father and uncle on a protracted business trip in the thirteenth century. But long before Marco Polo wrote of his adventures, merchants were conducting business in strange and exotic lands.

Business travel is as old as business itself. Records show that as far back as the seventh century A.D., the Silk Road (not one road, in fact, but many) was peopled by itinerant businesspeople plying their trade in everything from silk and spices to Buddhist scriptures. The city of Chang'an in China, the starting point of the great silk route, which stood where Xian is today, grew fat on the exploits of these early mercantile travelers. The 754 AD census of the city indicates that more than 5,000 foreigners were based in the city, from as far afield as India, Japan, and Malaysia. The route was a conduit for rare plants, medicines, and textiles that were traded in the city's bazaars. In those days, the representatives of the emperor took their pick of the goods before trade could commence. The emperors have gone, but the need to understand local traditions and comply with the relevant authorities remains integral to the business traveler's license to operate. Today navigating cultural nuances and national laws still requires a deep knowledge.

Why Travel?

The reality is that extensive traveling is a prerequisite for anyone in a top job who wants to help an organization maintain its competitive edge. "The winners are going to be those people who can connect and collaborate, at lightning speed, across markets, geographies, time zones, demographics, and more," says Kevin Roberts, worldwide CEO of global communications organization Saatchi & Saatchi. During one 12-month period, Roberts spent 175 nights in hotels on business travel.

Business relationships are based on communication—and, as we've seen, communication is the cornerstone of any top job. The question is, why have all the new communication media failed to make a dent in travel schedules? The answer seems to lie with a simple statistic. More than 80 percent of human communication is nonverbal (some studies put it as high as 93 percent). In other words, email, telephone, videoconferencing, and all the other communications marvels do not have the bandwidth to carry more than 20 percent of the face-to-face experience.

Facial expressions, body language, eye contact—these are key conduits. Without them, you can't get past first base. It's tough to bond over the Internet. So unless your client is in the next office, to do business, you have to travel. How else can you meet customers, colleagues, and competitors? "A CEO from Switzerland told me once that he has a personal key performance indicator that he wants to meet twice as many customers as investors, and I think that's a very good target," says Ribar.

At Caterpillar, Owens travels the world attending employee meetings. With more than 300 significant facilities scattered across 40 countries, it is impossible for him to visit every one every year, but he tries to ensure that an executive officer from headquarters in Peoria gets to every major facility. "That's a lot of getting out," he reflects, "but I like to be sure that at least one of us appears there and has a chance to have a dialogue and talk to people, make them feel like they're a critical part of our organization everywhere we do business."

The downsides of constant travel are well documented, and justifiably so. Less emphasized are the plus sides. As a well-traveled leader, you get to meet a huge number of people and develop relationships that are important to them as businesspeople and as human beings. Travel allows people to connect. It can be a richly rewarding personal experience. Travel not only broadens the expense account—business trips offer new and exciting vistas.

Surveys consistently show that young people entering the workforce regard travel as a perk. A survey of 350 Oxford University students in their final year of study, for example, sought to understand what motivates young people to join established firms. The survey found that foreign travel was among the factors the students valued most, surpassed only by achieving the right balance between work and leisure—and pay.

Loyal Supporters

With huge demands on your limited time and a punishing travel schedule, a leader needs support.

Many companies now have a chief operating officer (COO) who manages internally, while the CEO devotes more attention to what's going on outside. This is not a new idea; examples of famous business double acts abound. Think of David Hewlett and Bill Packard, James Hanson and Gordon White, Microsoft founders Bill Gates and Paul Allen, Body Shop's Gordon and Anita Roddick. Richard Branson relies on his sidekick of many years, Will Whitehorn. More recently, David Filo and Jerry Yang, the founders of Yahoo!, styled themselves chief Yahoos.

Stephen Miles, a partner in Leadership Consulting at Heidrick & Struggles, has done a lot of work on the role of the COO. He sounds a note of caution about the COO/CEO relationship in his book (coauthored with Nathan Bennett) *Riding Shotgun*. He notes, "The key ingredient for COO effectiveness is often whether the CEO is ready to share power. Unfortunately, some COOs do not realize the CEO is not ready until they are in the position and friction begins to appear in the relationship."

But most leaders today seem to understand that solo leadership in the corporate world is ultimately inefficient and ineffective—at least, they know this in theory. No one individual, no matter how gifted, can be right all the time; no one individual, particularly in a large organization, has the relevant information to make every important decision. Over time, resources become misallocated, opportunities are missed, and innovation becomes stifled. Overcontrol saps initiative, and bureaucratic behavior ensues.

"If you are working for a large firm, there are a number of tensions that managers deal with," says José Luis Álvarez, associate dean at the Instituto de Empresa Business School in Spain. "Paying attention to clients, paying attention to operations, paying attention to the outside or inside of the organization, paying attention to the future or to the present...you are focused on a strategy or on tactics. You are focused on control, or innovation; on numbers, or on people; on maintenance, or on change. There are so many dilemmas that no manager could cope with all of them—at least, not simultaneously. The more complex the organization, the more that power sharing makes sense."

Whether you like it or not, a leader has to rely on others—a secretary, a spouse, colleagues, a team, friends, a BlackBerry, and many more. If you fly solo, you go around in circles.

Role Models

In talking to leaders, I'm amazed by how much help and support they derive from early role models. McClure continues to cite the advice of one of his company's bankers, Gene Miller. "Gene said one of the things he learned early on was the responsibility which lay in his title, CEO," McClure says. "He said the C is for customers, the E is for employees, and the O is for owners. That's who I am responsible to. I have always carried that as my mantra. I've changed it a little bit and refer to it now as C^2EO because the second C to me is also the community. So I define my title as C^2EO, which is Customer, Community, Employees, and Owners."

For the past 30 years, Seung-Yu Kim of Hana Financial Group has had an epigram from Alfred P. Sloan mounted in a frame in his office: "The circumstances of the ever-changing market and ever-changing product are capable of breaking any business organization if that organization is unprepared for change." Sloan was the industry-shaping CEO of General Motors during its early development. The same wise words are mounted at the entrance of MIT's Sloan Management School to remind its students of the importance of markets, customers, and innovation.

"Only companies which foresee market trends and proactively confront them may lead the market, and the financial industry is not an exception," says Kim. "As Hana Bank rose to become one of Korea's big four financial groups, at every single crossroads, our people's efforts and mind-sets effectively corresponded to changes in the market and our customers' expectations. During my career, I have never forgotten Mr. Sloan's lesson and will cherish it for the rest of my service."

Apart from Sloan, Kim names Jung-Ho Kim, the head of the branch where he started his career in the finance industry, as another role model. "He was a leader with great discipline," Kim recalls. "A newcomer who could not calculate on an abacus had to come to the office by 7 AM and practice for an hour before our daily business. And after business hours, we had to attend classes held by junior managers. He always sat at the back and did not leave until the end of the class. Being the first to arrive and the last to leave, he even volunteered for chores such as separating old currencies. Sometimes his professionalism made some of us uncomfortable, but none of us doubted his leadership.

"I still remember him saying, 'The life of a banker lies in his honesty,' as I heard it so many times. Whenever we received incentive payments for our performance, he handed it to each of us and reminded us, 'You earned this with your hardships. Do not waste it. Save it.'" Kim worked under Jung-Ho Kim for a year before he was transferred to another branch. "But my memories of him stay with me," he says.

My role models are in the more distant past: the wisdom of Mahatma Gandhi and Abraham Lincoln, and the speeches of Theodore Roosevelt. I find one speech of Teddy Roosevelt's find particularly valuable. Speaking in Paris in 1910, Roosevelt said this:

> It is not the critic who counts: not the man who points out how the strong man stumbles or where the doer of deeds could have

done better. The credit belongs to the man who is actually in the arena, whose face is marred by dust and sweat and blood, who strives valiantly, who errs and comes up short again and again, because there is no effort without error or shortcoming, but who knows the great enthusiasms, the great devotions, who spends himself for a worthy cause; who, at the best, knows, in the end, the triumph of high achievement, and who, at the worst, if he fails, at least he fails while daring greatly, so that his place shall never be with those cold and timid souls who knew neither victory nor defeat.

That's pretty inspiring isn't it?

Personal Development

Another challenge amid all this is to develop your own skills. No one is perfect. Leaders also need to develop and improve. This is surprisingly difficult. It's a bit like trying to get fit when you are in the middle of a title fight.

In a world where knowledge is a critical organizational asset, great emphasis is placed on personal development. Corporate universities, e-learning programs, in-house training, personal learning networks— these are just a few of the learning options available to employees. But what is available for those higher up the organization? What about a CMO who wants to hone leadership skills, acquire a deeper self-knowledge, or maybe just retain the edge both mentally and physically?

The higher up you are, the harder it is to do personal development. For a start, who delivers it? When you get to the top of the organization, the issues you are dealing with revolve much more around leadership style, personal effectiveness, and interpersonal skills, such as empathy, communication, listening, impact, clarity. This is feedback and coaching that is very hard to give to anyone who is more senior than you or who is a colleague.

Externally, executive education programs and leadership forums are options. But many senior executives are too busy running teams and organizations to take the time out to attend.

Just a few years ago, news that a senior executive was using a coach would have raised eyebrows in the boardroom. Today, however, assigning an executive coach to improve a leader's management performance or overcome personal development deficiencies is a far more acceptable practice.

For senior executives, the attractions of employing a coach are obvious. There's no need to leave the office, for a start—a major plus for time-strapped executives. Better still, the coach fits into the executive's timetable and provides a tailor-made program focused solely on the needs of the executive.

Then there is the important issue of trust and confidentiality. "We have this idea of organizations as pyramids, so at the top there's only space for one person," says Álvarez. "Also, there are tactical reasons: Careers are individualistic, and people are just not prepared for or used to sharing power. People are not used to trusting someone." That's sad but true, yet trust underpins the coaching relationship. "An executive coach provides a safe place—who else can leaders turn to?" says one coach. "They are surrounded by senior managers who drink from the same water fountain."

I have three individuals, totally outside the company, whom I rely on and run ideas past. I find their impartial, often difficult advice an important safety valve.

Feeling Good, Doing Good, Having Fun

All of this makes sense only if there's a point to it all—the job, your organization, your career. This goes beyond simply making money for yourself and your employer. That's why corporate social responsibility

(CSR) is a key aspect of any approach to leading people. It is important on a number of levels, but it also allows people to have some fun.

You probably think it sounds a little trivial. I don't think so. We're talking about something that's a fundamental driver for the most talented people working at the cutting edge today, and that includes the senior team.

When talented people reach a certain level, they want something more than a paycheck as a reward; they want to feel that they make a difference. Feeling that you are making a contribution does a lot for your well-being.

Says Gary Knell of Sesame Workshop, "At the end of the day, you've got to have fun at this job. When this stops becoming something that you get up in the morning and are really enthusiastic about coming in to tackle every day, it's probably time to move on."

Importantly, having fun increases productivity. It makes people work harder, faster, and smarter. Firms that focus on fun are more productive. When companies show a commitment to something bigger than the profit motive, they build loyalty and show soul. Firms that focus on making fun a part of their culture build a better work/life balance, which, in turn, means healthier, more motivated employees. The same is true for those in top jobs, where CSR and philanthropy can provide a sense of purpose beyond hitting earnings targets.

To some, this sounds superficial, but I'm not alone in my genuine belief that CSR is an important aspect of any company's activities. Many other business leaders share this view. It's not just about doing good, though—it has to make sound business sense.

"You cannot be sustainable if you do not have the financial results which afford it," says Jacques Aigrain, CEO at Swiss Re. "It is being socially responsible in terms of being perfectly conscious of the social impact of your company. In our case, as we don't make goods, it's mainly an issue of making sure that we have the appropriate processes in place to ensure that we are not providing insurance services to activities which would not be viewed as socially responsible. So we have a sustainability committee which checks on the appropriate compatibilities of some activities."

This is CSR that goes to the heart of the business. "There is also a very clearly aligned interest on the climate issue, because climate change has a very direct influence on our business and economic model," says Aigrain. "We are very vocal and very involved in all matters relating to climate and, by symbiosis, on matters of water and the sustainability of water supplies. It's not just because we think it's lovely charity-oriented talk, but because it's highly compatible with and essential for our business model. So it means being very involved in the debate, sponsoring a number of research projects, participating in the awareness campaigns, and being highly visible in building awareness of the macroeconomic challenge related to climate change."

Different Strokes for Different Folks

Ask leaders how they factor in some downtime, and you'll get a bunch of different answers. One they will all tell you, though, is that, even if (*especially* if) you are a global CEO, you still need to take some time out to unwind, both physically and mentally.

"Careers are very jerky. People make huge contributions at various points in their career, and they have a lot of time off," observes Carl Schramm of the Kaufmann Foundation, who is a voracious reader in his downtime. "Winston Churchill is a classic example, and he's a fantastic inspiration. He led by ideas and endured a period when people just would not talk to him. And he saw the world so clearly. He had the courage of his convictions."

One CFO told me about visiting another corporation where busyness reigned supreme. "Every day there were two or three firmwide new initiatives. Everybody had open calendars. The entire day, nine hours a day, was controlled by somebody else. People had to go to meetings, but they didn't know what they were about. People were bombarded with ideas that weren't screened. If you wanted to manage your career up, you had to invest three or four hours a day just catching up with the news in the company. You can't manage a company like that. You overload."

Aigrain is a strong believer in taking some "thinking" time away from the everyday pressures of the job. "Is it possible to switch off between work and home and home and work? I think it's critical. As the CEO, you must take some distance from the day-to-day affairs and be able to focus on strategic matters, including people issues and the strategic direction of competitors, the market, yourself, and your company. That means that there are moments when you will be utterly absorbed in issues which are a little more practical and short term.

"I'm lucky enough that, 50 meters from my home I'm in the forest. I try to exercise every day, and that's usually my best time for thinking, refreshing, and finding a new angle on issues that I'm trying to deal with. That quality time, even though it's a limited number of hours with your husband or wife (or partner), with your kids, is also absolutely essential for finding the right balance.

"Because one of the results of being 'wired' all the time is that you end up being disconnected from the real world."

Key Points

- Ultimately, as the leader of an organization or part of an organization, you must retain a healthy perspective on work/life balance, despite all the pressures of the job and its undoubted importance in terms of the organization. Leaders should remember that they are in a privileged position. It might seem that so many people want a piece of them that there's nothing left to give—but there is always a little bit extra.

- Getting the balance right demands that you travel when needed by the business, and travel healthily. It also requires that you maximize support networks and develop new skills as your career develops.

Resources

Álvarez, José Luis, and Silviya Svejenova. *Sharing Executive Power* (New York: Cambridge University Press, 2005).

Bennett, Nathan, and Stephen A. Miles. *Riding Shotgun: The Role of the COO* (Stanford, CA: Stanford Business Books, 2006).

Crainer, Stuart, and Des Dearlove. *Financial Times Guide to Business Travel* (London: Financial Times/Pearson Education, 2001).

Fast Company/Roper Starch Worldwide. "How Much Is Enough?" *Fast Company* 26 (June 1999): 108.

Goldsmith, Marshall (with Mark Reiter). *What Got You Here Won't Get You There* (New York: Hyperion, 2007).

National Sleep Foundation. *Less Fun, Less Sleep, More Work: An American Portrait*. NSF, 27 March 2001.

The CEO Report. FTdynamo, 2001.

Worrall, Les, and Cary L. Cooper. "Working Patterns and Working Hours: Their Impact on U.K. Managers." *Leadership and Organization Development Journal* 20 (1999): 6–10.

8

Trials, Tribulations, and Triumphs

What are the good things about occupying a top job? What are the worst?

"While I am thinking about the company's long-term direction, it is vital for me to remain in touch with the current reality."

—*Carlos Ghosn, president and CEO, Nissan and Renault*

Only Validate

After talking with leaders about their leadership theories and approaches to top jobs, I wanted to look at the day-to-day work and find out which issues really dogged them—the irritations, the worries, and also the pleasures.

"A good day for me is when I see healthy conflict inside the company," Carlos Ghosn confided. "The solutions to all problems can be found inside the company, and I am encouraged when I see Nissan teams worldwide leveraging all the resources and talent available to them to create value. This gives me an indication that people are learning and the company is in a healthy state."

Jacques Aigrain, CEO of Swiss Re, had a more personal view: "The best bit of the job is undoubtedly the fact that you suddenly realize, although maybe not in the first few months, that you can truly influence a large, long-established organization. You can see it change from a practical standpoint, from a people's behavior standpoint, and from a dynamic and eventually result standpoint, much faster than you would have imagined....You see that your efforts are not going to waste."

Aigrain is right. Leaders change organizations and can shape people's behavior, expectations, and lives. Other top jobbers took delight in more fundamental achievements. "I am a recent CEO [18 months], but what I am most satisfied about is probably the mobilization of the whole organization on safety," says Bruno Lafont, chairman and CEO of Lafarge. "Safety is at the heart of our values—an organization like Lafarge must ensure the safety of its employees and contractors. Lafarge is already the best in its sector, but we want to join best-in-class industrial companies. I am deeply convinced that excellence in safety is leading to performance excellence overall. Each of our employees is now fully empowered in this effort, and this is something that has a strong value for our group."

Of course, it would be wrong to overlook the frustrating, depressing, and even downright bad bits that leaders occasionally experience. "I was never late, my whole life, until I got this job," one senior executive lamented in conversation. The job can break the habits of a lifetime. "The thing I did wrong initially was watching the stock price too much," another leader confided.

Politics also stands in the way at times. "The [most unpleasant] part of the job is the requirement to cajole and gently prod, again, again, and again, people at various levels of the organization, who tend to make changes or processes or adjustments, or even business opportunities, more politically loaded than need be," says Aigrain. "You end up playing politics to help things get back. It's a waste of time."

Truth be told, some people in every organization will get in the way in some way. The political nature of human beings is an occupational hazard for leaders. "Being busy doesn't bother me at all—the worst part of my job is individuals who see a crystal-clear, calm pond and then throw a stone in it, just to see the ripples," one executive told me. "It takes up time and disrupts the organization—some individuals, for whatever reason, think that's their reason in life."

People are a repeated theme in any gathering of leaders. Skinner got some good advice from an old personnel manager years ago while standing in the parking lot in an old part of Chicago: "He said, 'Listen, be your own man.' And I take that to mean that I work for the brand. Sometimes that means you have to disagree with the leadership, with the boss. Sometimes it's painful. Sometimes you could even lose your job, I suppose, but I think it needs to be done for you to be most effective."

Good leaders also have to do their homework when picking candidates, the people they'll surround themselves with. "One time I could have had any person I wanted in a particular job," recalls Skinner. "I was in Pittsburgh, and the president of the company told me [I could] have anybody [I wanted]. So I reached out for a guy by reputation. I didn't do my homework and didn't talk to three or four other people about the job, which I think is mandatory. And I got the wrong guy. It was the biggest mistake I ever made. He was terrible."

Changed Perceptions

It's not just your perception of people; it is how they see you. Suddenly, in a top job, you seem different—to others, at least. The reality is that when you take on a top job, relationships and expectations change. Seung-Yu Kim, CEO of Korea's Hana Financial Group, told me a very moving story about a close friend of his. They had graduated from high school together, and their families knew each other. "We were hand and glove," Kim remembers.

Kim's friend's family ran a business that manufactured school uniforms. After graduation, Kim's friend succeeded his father to run the company. Then the Korean government suddenly changed the law on the wearing of school uniforms. The business needed to change and began looking at manufacturing fashionable clothing.

With his corporate experience, Kim realized that such a change of business was risky and counseled against it. Manufacturing school uniforms and fashionable clothing required different know-how and distribution channels, among other things. He tried to dissuade his friend, but his friend did not listen.

Soon afterward, sales fell and the company's cash flow dried up. Kim's friend eventually came asking for some short-term operating capital. Kim refused his request: "There was no guarantee that his business would recover even if I provided some credit as a stopgap," Kim explains. "My friend desperately asked for my help, relying on our long-time friendship, and he was enraged at my refusal. After a few weeks, I heard that his company was insolvent and eventually he was imprisoned. Afterward, I asked myself hundreds of times why I had to choose this profession, which caused me and my best friend to leave each other like that."

A few years later, Kim got a call from one of the local Hana Bank branch managers. He said that a friend of Kim's had visited the branch and asked him to deliver an invitation to the wedding of the friend's daughter. Kim recalled that this friend had gone to prison because Kim had refused to help him. Kim cancelled everything in his schedule and rushed to meet him.

"There I found my friend standing at his daughter's wedding to welcome guests," Kim says. "I knew I owed him an apology, but he was the first one to talk. Grabbing my hands, he said, 'Now I understand. Maybe I would have made the same choice as you had if I had been in your position.' I couldn't say anything. We just hugged each other. I know I was lucky to recover my relationship with my friend after all. But the feelings I had to go through were the worst, though they are commonly shared by those in the financial industry."

Lemonade?

Talking to leaders, I've found that the biggest day-to-day challenge and irritant is rewarding people. Rose tackled this at Marks & Spencer, which had previously rewarded people for the length of their service instead of their performance. The organization now has a series of incentives and performance-related plans in place. Says Rose, "Old Marks & Spencer would have said, 'Blame the management.' Now we say, 'Blame yourself: If you didn't get a bonus, you didn't earn it. If your colleagues aren't getting a bonus, you let them down.'" Quite rightly, this policy goes all the way down the staff, to the checkout girl who gets a £500 bonus because she met her service levels to the store, because she gave the customer a smile, because she sold more volume, because customer letters now all say that the service is so much better. "And if 55,000 or 50 of our customer assistants do that every day, we'll all get rich," Rose says. "And if they don't, then we're stuffed."

This issue was brought home to me on a family holiday. Every summer we go to North Carolina. Sitting on the front porch after a day at the beach, my daughter and some of her friends thought it would be fun to make some lemonade and then set up a stand selling it at the front of the garden. The team was galvanized. Lemonade was made, a table dragged out, marketing materials created (by crayon), and the cash began to pour in. At 50¢ per glass, it was attractively priced for parched customers on their way back from the beach. The kids all stood around excitedly as the first few people parted with their money. We sat back with parental pride at their business acumen and enthusiasm.

Five minutes later, a few of the kids had drifted off. The marketing team members were now chasing a butterfly. The pricing strategist was playing in the sand, and others were dispersed around the garden doing what kids do. My daughter carried on gamely selling lemonade.

A couple hours later, the lemonade was exhausted and the money was added up: $12. My daughter asked everyone who had helped to stand in line to be paid. Everyone suddenly materialized. The marketers gave up on their butterfly, the pricing strategist abandoned the sand, and the garden looked a whole lot less interesting. They stood in line and held out their hands.

And that is how we are in organizations. We stand in line and hold out our hands for our bonuses. And if we don't get our share, we kick up a fuss, even if we have been off with the butterflies.

This was brought home to me when I met up with a friend who works for a leading investment bank. Now, they know a thing or two about bonuses, but the same principles applied. He told me that a guy who got a $19 million bonus (he must have sold a lot of lemonade) was unhappy because he didn't get $19.2 million. Seriously, why not $20 million or $21 million? Why the 0.2?

People holding out their hands is a big issue for leaders. Around 30 percent of people change jobs because they want to be paid more. This group takes up a lot of top exec time. This is an issue I have tried to manage myself. Early in my time at Heidrick & Struggles, I sent this email to all our staff:

> Hi everyone,
>
> I like Fridays for two reasons:
>
> **1.** The weekend is here and we can celebrate a great week.
>
> or
>
> **2.** The weekend is here and we can say goodbye to a bad week.
>
> Personally, I have had a great week and learned a lot. I spent the first three days in Moscow, a fantastic city, if you have a chance to visit—full of opportunity (and we have a very strong team there). While in Moscow, I met a number of leaders, but one particular meeting sticks in my mind: It was with the CEO of a leading global bank.

The day of our meeting happened to be bonus day for this bank, and he was a little on edge. We talked about how he was feeling and, in particular, the build-up of the past six to eight weeks. He spoke about the need to "manage expectations," wondering about retention issues and whether individuals would walk.

His firm had been acquired by this big global bank, so it was not about him; it was about his genuine concern for his people. He told me, "When I owned my firm, bonuses were decided on Wednesday and paid the following Monday. The wait is what kills you—compensation is so emotive and people stir each other up, endlessly predicting what might or might not happen.

"It's amazing to watch," he said, "because you get to a point where people can't separate fact from fiction—I am glad this will soon be over."

The point of me sharing this with you is that we are approximately five weeks away from paying bonuses. And guess what? This year, like most others, will be emotional—maybe even more so because of the changes we have made:

- Moving to a single payment
- Overhauling the comp system
- Working to reunify the firm

Change is something we all talk about but none of us seems too good at—and in times of change, individuals always seem to think the worst.

So how can we make things better? Well, we all have choices. As individuals, we can choose to thrive on the angst of the compensation roller coaster for the next few weeks, *or* we can recognize, as an organization, that the leadership of the firm wants to take care of its people—and will endeavor to do so.

Now, will there be individuals who we think will be happy that will be unhappy?

Absolutely.

Will there be individuals who we think will be unhappy that will be happy?

Absolutely.

In our firm of more than 1,685 people, will we make a few mistakes?

Absolutely.

And in this way we are no different from most organizations.

I promise that we will do the best we can possibly do to recognize all those people who have contributed to the organization. It already looks like we've had a great start to the year: The global market is buoyant, and I expect us to build on our successes in January month by month.

So for those of you who had a great week, go celebrate. For those of you who had a bad week, go celebrate the fact that the week is over. Either way, have a great weekend.

Kevin

Clock Watching

The other big issue leaders bring up repeatedly is time. As we have seen, for leaders and many others in today's organizations, time is at a premium. Your days are mapped out for you with barely a few minutes' leeway. Then a colleague approaches you and whispers, "Can I have five minutes?" Of course, you want to give someone time. That's why you're there. You want to listen and talk. You want people's ideas. You want to hear their worries and hopes.

But the reality is that five minutes is never five minutes. It is usually 30 minutes, often an hour. Multiply those five minutes by the number of employees around the world, and not much time remains in your career, let alone the work week.

Leaders all have a different approach to this. What unifies them is a sense that time is like gold dust: It had better be well used.

One leader with even more pressures than normal is Carlos Ghosn, responsible for Nissan and Renault. "There are two ways I operate," he explained to me. "One is at a very high level. Being a CEO of two companies, I have learned to empower based on a clear, unique, shared strategy. I screen decisions. If an executive can solve the problem, let him or her solve the problem. Coming to the CEO would be a waste of time. The principle of empowerment allows that only the toughest problems and the toughest decisions come to the CEO. Enabling decisions to be [made] at the lowest level possible in the company can increase speed and gain precision."

On another level, Ghosn says, he wants to remain in touch with reality. "I spend as much time as I can [visiting] the *gemba*, the people on the shop floors, to listen to their opinions and see if there is anything that can be improved and implemented at the company level. This interaction allows me to stay in tune with what is going on in the company. People know that when I visit, I am there not for protocol, but to spend time with them, to hear their opinions and feelings, to praise them for their achievements, and to encourage them in their challenges. When I go there, I fully engage myself with the team. Doing this allows me to keep myself focused on what is real."

Richard Baker of Alliance Boots has developed his own unique approach. He is disciplined and doesn't allow meetings to run over. "I have found a good rhythm which works for me," he says. "You have to be ruthlessly well organized. I rarely cancel a meeting. I remember being a middle manager and people above changing their diaries. I am very punctual. If the CEO is disorganized, there is a knock-on effect. If I was highly flexible or not punctual, it would be chaos."

Baker also makes deliveries with one of his company's trucks. It's amazing how many ways leaders manage to spend time with their people and their customers. When he has a couple free hours, McClure instructs his assistant to block off time so he can walk around the technology center, among other parts of the company. "I just walk through, stick my head into an engineer's cubicle, and ask them what they're doing," he says. "The excitement and enthusiasm that I get from listening to our engineers is really infectious." McClure also goes to the company's experimental garage, where engineers do a lot of work for customers, and spends time with the techs. A couple weeks ago, he even joined in a small cake-and-coffee celebration for three techs who got their commercial drivers' licenses. "Recognition, no matter how small, goes a long way—and that is important to me," McClure says. "My wife can tell when I've been either to a plant or in one of our engineering centers because I'll come home with a different level of enthusiasm. It's this kind of excitement that tells me this is the future of the company. We've got some young, bright engineers, and it's amazing to see the kind of things they can do."

Listening Intently

Another thing leaders commonly hear, though usually not directly, is that they don't listen to people's gripes. I was reminded of this when I spoke with Patrick Swygert. He told me about the extraordinary experience of meeting Nelson Mandela: "When I met him, two things were obvious to me. One, he appeared to be listening to what I had to say…. I was incredibly flattered. Then second, in his response, it was clear he had listened to what I had to say, and I said to myself, 'Well, I'll follow this guy anywhere. He is giving me the benefit of listening to me and digesting what I say. What a compliment! [He's] a world-wide figure, a charismatic personality, who doesn't need to hear what I have to say, but he's clever and empathetic enough, and enough of a leader, to both listen and let me know he's listening.'" Mandela then began to talk about his vision for a free South Africa in simple declaratory sentences. "It was obvious that he meant what he said and he said it well," says Swygert. "So now he's listened to me, and he's told me something about where he'd like to go. Well, I want to be next to this guy; I don't want to leave him. And I think that's something that some people have, and some people do not."

Nelson Mandela can listen, but his greatness and that of other leaders does not lie simply in listening; it lies in listening, giving your own opinion, and then taking action. People might complain that you, their boss, don't listen, but the reality is that you do listen—and then you make a decision. And if the decision is not what they want or have advised, they accuse you of not listening. This point was brought home to me when I heard Tony Blair observe, "The hardest thing about leadership is learning to ignore the loudest voices."

Who Is Everyone?

Another frequently heard warning sign for the leader is being told, "Everyone thinks this" or "That's what everyone is saying." You must constantly pin down who this *everyone* is. They are often mythical.

On this point, I frequently tell a story about four people named Everybody, Somebody, Anybody, and Nobody.

> An important job had to be done, and Everybody was asked to do it. Everybody was sure Somebody would do it. Anybody could have done it, but Nobody did it.
>
> Somebody got angry about that because it was Everybody's job. Everybody thought Anybody could do it, but Nobody realized that Everybody wouldn't do it.
>
> It ended up that Everybody blamed Somebody when Nobody did what Anybody could have done.

Any manager running any organization will recognize this story.

It Really Is About People

For me, the triumphs of the job are always connected to people— for example, a consultant in Europe calling me when I had taken over running his area and saying, "This is the first time in ten years that I have been proud to be a member of this firm."

Time and time again, leaders have told me that the best thing about their job is the people. They're spot on. It is those moments when either you see people grow or do something great—get a big bit of business, get a big pitch—or someone you've hired gets promoted and is doing really well.

As Gerry Roche of Heidrick & Struggles says, "A good manager is a mentor to all his people. Now, it can be dicey if your mentor is someone other than the person to whom you report. Reporting to Manager A and being mentored by Manager B requires good communication and trust."

Key Points

- Being a leader is different. People see you differently, and their expectations of you change.
- Topping the complaints for leaders are matters of rewards and remuneration. How you approach these issues and actively manage them is the key to success.
- Then there's the lack of time. Your only hope for managing your time is to hire a great assistant, manage meetings ruthlessly, and refuse to be blindsided by requests for a quick five-minute discussion.
- The paradox is that although you have to ration your time rigorously, you have to spend a lot of time listening. None of this time is ever wasted—even if you choose to eventually ignore what you have heard.
- In the final analysis, successful leaders are great at managing people. This is the job.

9

Tomorrow's Leaders

What are the characteristics of the 2020 leader? What skills and capabilities do you need to develop if you are to make the golden career leap into a top job?

"What advice would you give somebody who aspired to be a CEO in the future? It would be to have conviction. You need passion and conviction, but you also need to be ready to adjust it for the human dimension. You may have a design, but you will have to play with the hand of cards that you have: your people."

—*Jacques Aigrain, CEO, Swiss Re*

Chief Entrepreneurial Officers

The Kauffman Foundation develops innovative ideas to promote entrepreneurship and, over four decades, has become one of the largest foundations in the United States, with assets of approximately $2 billion. The president and CEO of the foundation, Carl Schramm, trained as an economist and lawyer and, for a time, worked in academia. His career evolved as he took on leadership roles with companies in the healthcare and insurance industries. An entrepreneur in his own right, Schramm was involved in numerous start-up ventures before he was chosen as the CEO of Kauffman. The foundation, based in Kansas City, Missouri, was created by Ewing Kauffman, who went from salesman to founder of a pharmaceutical company that started in the basement of his home.

Schramm paints a powerful picture of the world that leaders will have to manage tomorrow and the skills they will need as a result. "Seventy percent of college kids want to work for themselves. That's fantastic. When I got out of college, you'd have four jobs between 22 and 65. I've got a son coming out of college next year. He's 22, and he'll have four jobs by the time he's 30. The chances are very high he'll work for himself in one of those four, or work with somebody he knows in college. And by the time he's 40, he will have had ten jobs."

Schramm predicts a more freewheeling entrepreneurial environment: "Some people are hedgehogs and some people are foxes. Foxes are innovators; hedgehogs, oddly, I think, are entrepreneurs. People see entrepreneurs with lightning bolts going through their heads all the time, but I don't think that's right at all. I think the job of the entrepreneur is to take one good idea, settle it down, make the matrix work, and deliver the product. A lot of our leaders grow up in cultures in large corporations where they talk about entrepreneurship, but they still hunt these entrepreneurs down and knock them off because they are disturbing inside companies."

The Loyalty Question

The need for more freewheeling entrepreneurial leaders is emerging already. It is arising because the nature of our relationship with our employers has changed. Takeshi Niinami, CEO of Lawson in Japan, reflects that, of his intake of 200 into Mitsubishi, 160 still work with Mitsubishi or Mitsubishi subsidiaries. "Loyalty is the real issue for Mitsubishi, for big companies," he says. "The younger generation wants to challenge at an early stage. They don't want to wait until they are 42 or 43 to become a general manager. For example, at Mitsubishi, if you want to be an executive, they say you have to wait until age 54.

Before then, a lot of people get out and take opportunities to make themselves more capable in the market."

The challenge for organizations now is that the next generation of senior executives may be motivated by factors other than the benefits package. Not only will they be seeking better work/life balance and more career flexibility, but they are likely to be looking just as hard for the opportunity and space to express their individuality. Now, that is a challenge.

Tomorrow's leaders will be a lot more demanding of themselves and their organizations. Says Schramm, "Every single kid implicitly is brand-managing themselves. They're making a calculation every single day about the brand equity that they're building today. They're going to stay at IBM just as long as IBM continues to contribute to their brand equity, because that's their brand security. This is a real challenge for businesses in the future. The days of Michael Porter and the Strategic Retreat in November at a golf course with people from McKinsey telling you the future of your company are over. The 25-year-olds from engineering school have to be part of the whole dream."

The conclusion? Simple, says Schramm: "There's only one issue of the future: managing people."

Tomorrow's Leaders

To better understand this new generation, I looked at research into high-flying leaders by London's Cass Business School and business writer Steve Coomber. This revealed a startling disparity in the ages of high-performing leaders across the globe. It also highlighted the executive stars of the future, listing the top 50 global high-flying leaders under the age of 45.

The study, which looked at the 52-week return on share prices of more than 1,500 companies listed on the world's major stock exchanges, relies on efficient market theory, which states that, in a perfect world, in a perfect market, the share price of a company should reflect all information known about that company. Movements in share prices were used as an indicator of what the markets—and, therefore, the leaders—thought about particular companies.

Instead of comparing companies in different regions directly, the returns were adjusted to account for local market movements by considering how a particular stock outperformed the local market. The top performers were leaders who managed to outperform their local market by an impressive margin.

The first surprise in the research results is the lack of young leaders in the United States. There was no CEO under 40 in the S&P 500. Across the world, the average age of a CEO was 54, and the most common age 57. This echoes the findings of past corporate surveys. In 1995, a Booz Allen Hamilton survey of the 2,500 largest publicly traded corporations revealed the average starting age of a CEO to be just over 50.

The youngest CEO in the survey was 29-year-old Sahba Abedian of Sunland, the Australian property group, the only CEO under 30. A further 5 were under 35, and 19 more under 40. Although there were only 25 leaders under 40, it was not all bad news for executives planning a swift route to the top.

Perhaps the most interesting results are those showing the rise of a cadre of young leaders in China. Eight of the top ten leaders in the ranking, and 14 of the top 20, lead companies listed in China. Nearly half (23) of the top 50 leaders under the age of 45 are from China. The youngest is 33, and 12 are 40 or younger.

The Chinese leaders head up some of the global corporate giants of the future. The top-ranked CEO on the list, Bin Zhao (aged 34), runs Shanghai Aero Auto Electromechanical (SAAE). The company gets over 80 percent of its revenue from auto parts and is also involved in satellite development. Turnover for 2005 was CNY 1.8 billion

($225.7 million), while net profit guidance for the first half of 2006 was up 300 percent on 2005 at CNY 13.2 million ($1.6 million).

"The old argument is that age brings experience and wisdom, qualities that help produce good performance," says Neil Beasley, the Cass MBA student who conducted the research. "If true, you would expect to see a link between older people performing better than younger people. Almost across the board, that link wasn't present. If they have got the skills, and they are in the right place at the right time, younger leaders can perform just as well as those with 10 or 20 years' more experience."

To sum up all of this, I spoke to my colleague Steve Tappin. "I believe that the next generation of leaders is going to be more like corporate entrepreneurs," Tappin told me. "They'll have worked and managed, been MDs of significant businesses, that will be international in nature, that will have complexity—and at the same time, they'll have spent some periods in a young, high-growth businesses as well, and may have spent some time in start-ups and private equity. So I think the new generation of leaders won't come from the traditional career path—I think that's over (Oxford, ICI, BP, MBA). I think there'll be a lot more people who have switched and have had different experiences."

Greater Diversity

Current leaders are already detecting the winds of change. There is no question that the leader of the future is likely to be younger, more entrepreneurial, more aware of their own brand, and more likely to reflect the increased diversity of globalization.

"The word that I like today around the leader's job, and the most important thing, is transparency," says Jim Skinner of McDonald's, "transparency in your relationships with your vendors and constituents, and whoever your customers are, and transparency around all that you have relationships with. You know, if you tell the truth, you don't have to try to remember what you said. Transparency around your model is why I think we've been so successful. We are a company with integrity. We deserve to be trusted. And you can only enhance that by thinking about transparency in everything you do. It's really a safe place to be as a CEO in the twenty-first century."

I asked Bruno Lafont, chairman and CEO of Lafarge, what qualities he thought the leader of the future would need to succeed. "I think he/she will need to have an even stronger international experience—in particular, it will probably be key that he/she has been exposed to Asia during his or her career," Lafont says. "He or she will need to have a strong leadership and to be an excellent communicator, to clarify the vision and the strategy as much as possible, in a world that is getting more and more complex. I think he or she will be closer to people and to the business on the ground than leaders could be in the past, because everything is becoming more global but also much more local."

Jacques Aigrain, CEO of Swiss Re, agrees that India and China are critical considerations: "Logically, there may be more Chinese and Indian and fewer American leaders; that's a pure characteristic of world economic changes. In a recent visit to our office in Beijing, seeing the level of enthusiasm and quality of the young Chinese that we have in the office, the challenge and opportunity is that, in 20 years' time, maybe the CEO of Swiss Re should be one of them. It would be the logical development. So that's thinking truly globally and truly about the evolution of our world as something that has become very small and unified."

I asked Nissan's Carlos Ghosn what he considered the skills demands on leaders of the future. His response begins with a sense of responsibility for your actions: "You cannot lead people in the twenty-first century if somehow you do not assume the consequence of your actions. And the consequence of your actions cannot be simply saying, 'I made a mistake.' No. From time to time, you have a vision, you have a plan, you have a strategy, you have an objective. You are asking people to work day and night for them, and you have to assume that personally. That is the management of the twenty-first century."

Ghosn believes that a company president must make the toughest problems or the toughest fronts priorities. He or she has to be someone who clarifies and makes the most difficult decisions. Then the president must be sure to be in the most risky places, showing up and supporting people on the front lines.

"Another increasingly important skill needed in this century is the ability to create value and strength out of diversity, not out of coherence and uniformity. The identity of the corporation is global. You need to know how people from different continents, cultures, and experiences can work in a very effective way to provide something meaningful and to compete against much more coherent organizations that are monocultural. If you can manage this, you will create a definite competitive advantage because diversity always brings more innovative ideas and wealth to the company, even though it is harder to manage."

Talent Spotting

A decade ago, three McKinsey consultants famously declared a war for talent. I was in Asia recently when a CEO stood up at dinner and said, "Good news, the war for talent is over. Talent won."

I believe there is a new war: the war to serve that talent. What is clear today is that talent is creating new markets. Whether it's hedge funds, private equity, technology, or creative industries, these are microeconomies dreamt up by the sheer power of imagination. From new markets in the geographies of eastern Europe to the fledgling economies of Asia, talent is spawning new ideas and new concepts. Recently at Heidrick & Struggles, we have picked up a search for a CIO (chief intellectual officer), a CSO (chief security officer), and a CSR (chief social responsibility officer). All brand new roles are dictated by the needs of today's talent on a swiftly tilting planet. Half of these jobs didn't exist five years ago.

What will happen by the time our children hit the workforce? Some evidence suggests that people from generation Y/generation iPod, or whatever digital epithet they are labeled with, are looking for something more than money. For a start, they're seeking better work/life balance and more career flexibility, and judging by their MySpace and Facebook pages, they want the ability to express their individuality, surely a challenge for any organization.

At the other end of the spectrum, the population is ageing. Over the next 25 years, there will be 75 million fewer Europeans and 65 million fewer Japanese. What does all this tell us? Simply that tomorrow will be different—as different as 1980 was from today, if not more so. Tomorrow is going to be as different as today's talent can imagine it to be.

This all leaves the leader of the future in a more complicated role than ever. "The days of the iron-fisted, iron-willed outsized personality leader are gone—those individuals have gone the way of the dinosaurs," says Patrick Swygert of Howard University. "For the CEO of the future, it's going to take incredible flexibility. Governance is going to be so radically different 5 years from now—not 10 or 15 or 20. It's going to take an agile CEO to wade through internal and external governance issues, and deal with globalization and regulation while keeping a strategic eye out for opportunities and challenges for the business. I think it's going to be an increasingly challenging position." In truth, it always was, but the challenges just got bigger.

Key Points

- The leaders of tomorrow will be younger. They will be more entrepreneurial, and their loyalty will be to themselves and their own brand—Brand You, as business guru Tom Peters puts it.
- They will embrace diversity and have to get used to incredible levels of complexity.
- Finding such talented individuals will become an ever-more-pressing issue in the world's boardrooms.

Resources

Beasley, Neil, and Steve Coomber. "The Top 50 Up and Coming Leaders." *CEO Magazine* (September 2006): 12–18.

Lucier, Chuck, Steven Wheeler, and Rolf Hobbel "CEO Succession 2006: The Era of the Inclusive Leader," Booz Allen's annual CEO succession study. *Strategy+Business* 47 (Summer 2007).

Michaels, Ed, Helen Handfield-Jones, and Beth Axelrod. *The War for Talent* (Boston: Harvard Business School Press, 2001).

Wooldridge, Adrian. "The Battle for Brainpower." *The Economist*, 5 October 2006.

10

The Life Beyond

Nothing lasts forever. Today's magazine-cover exec super-star is tomorrow's corporate footnote. But how does this affect leaders when they're in the job, and how can they prepare for the life beyond?

> "It is a tough job. It's better in the rearview mirror. Like climbing a mountain, it's not enjoyable every minute. You are endlessly overcoming problems, but it's great when you reach the summit."
>
> —*Richard Baker, CEO, Alliance Boots*

Tough Going

No one ever said it was going to be easy. Indeed, the CEO really earns his or her spurs when the going gets tough. Ask Carlos Ghosn, president and CEO of Nissan and Renault: "As a CEO, your performance cannot be judged merely when the company is successful and in good shape. This is not meaningful. No, your performance should also be judged by what you demonstrate when you are in a hole, when you are in trouble. Then you are going to be tested on your values. What are the things you believe in? What you are going to give away? What will you stand for even if more sacrifices are required? This is the real demonstration of the things you believe in."

I absolutely agree with this. I have an unidentified quote pinned to my office bulletin board that reminds me of what Ghosn is talking about:

> At decisive moments, leadership is about moving against the stream, asking yourself not what the people want right now, but rather what the people need in the long term and what should be done about it now. It's not easy; leadership has its risks. But when leaders aren't ready to lead, many other people have to pay the price.

Ghosn continues: "In Nissan in 1999 and 2000, what we stood for was obvious. We eliminated everything we did not stand for, and we kept everything we believed in. In a certain way, the results we are getting today and will get in the future can be considered the reward or punishment for what we have done or did not do.

"The challenge is in motivating people when you are going to restructure the company, close plants, reduce headcounts, dismantle keiretsu, dismantle cross-shareholding. You can understand the contradiction and why a lot of people cannot go through the process of change easily. Sometimes people go brutally into what they have to do, neglecting others' motivation, and they end up with a disaster." Ghosn goes on to give an example, "Cost reduction can build up a company if it is motivating, if it is within a purpose, if it points people toward an attractive destination, and if they understand the reason why they have to go through a difficult period. But if nobody invests in them to show them the purpose, and if they do not have the impression that they own the process, then cost reduction can be extremely destructive. This was one of our most challenging experiences in reviving Nissan."

Sell-By Dates

Tough times need to be faced with the sure knowledge that any crisis might be your last. Nothing lasts forever—although sometimes it feels as if it might. Sidney Harman, who runs Harman International

Industries, is 85 years old and still going strong. The head of Viacom is almost that age. In the past year or so, several older leaders have been pressed back into service. Gerry Grinstein was brought in at Delta at the age of 71. John Reed was no kid when he went to the New York Stock Exchange.

Perhaps more galling than being out of a job is that when you leave, you might just have set up the next guy to succeed. Look at Carly Fiorina. Hewlett-Packard is now enthusiastically reaping the benefits of her strategy.

Even so, leaders are surprisingly honest about how long they are likely to stay in the job. They are realistic almost to a fault.

Monika Ribar of Panalpina told me, "I am absolutely convinced that I am, for the time being, the absolute right person for this job here. But I'm not sure if I will still be in five years. You see, the company is always changing. Normally, when we have to replace somebody...we tend just to look for a copy of the predecessor, which is not necessarily the best person for the time being, and especially for the next five years. Our company really needed strong leadership and clear targets because that was missing in the past, but in five years' time, the company might need a much more sales-oriented person than I am."

Leaders are honest because they see themselves as stewards of the organization. The organization is bigger than they are. When this balance is out of kilter—when the leader's ego takes over—you begin to have problems.

Time and time again, the leaders I speak to talk about stewardship and what they will leave behind, their legacy. Typical of their sentiments are these of Gary Knell: "You've got to keep long-term stewardship in mind. [I try to] project how I would feel if I was not the CEO but I was on the board. What would I ask the CEO? What objective criteria would I use to evaluate his or her performance? I think by putting yourself in their position, you can have a more objective mirror on your own performance and whether you're really making a positive impact on the organization and maximizing your potential as an executive."

Being realistic also is important, says Knell. "The reality is, you're going to be able to lead less than a handful of important changes at the end of the day—directional changes of the company, maybe about a new line of business or maybe a new part of the world that you've engaged in. But there's not going to be more than five, and I think you're going to find two or three things that people will remember you by, even if you do a great job. It's about remembering that long-term stewardship is about moving an organization and leaving a legacy of change that will, in the long run, really help the organization prepare itself for the next generation of leadership."

Your Legacy

Seung-Yu Kim of Hana Financial Group also thinks of himself as a temporary steward of the company. "This is your company, not my company," he tells employees. "My tenure is only three years, and the shareholders decide whether they are going to re-elect me. But your tenure is 58 years, so it is your company, not mine."

Takeshi Niinami, CEO of Lawson, told me that part of his job was to understand the company's history. This was something he worked at. "I learned about the history of Lawson in detail, from reading reports and also listening to people who had retired and who were going to retire. The company history is important because that's the legacy. By understanding the history, it also helps you prepare for the future."

The future is always on the leader's mind. "Leaders have to see the future; they can't celebrate together with other executives when things go well today," lamented one CEO. Where is the company going? What does the CEO want to leave behind? "I think my vision is that, after my departure, maybe five or six or even three years after, people will see my role as great. Because what I left is the people, that's why the company can enjoy—a legacy of great people," says Niinami.

What Got You Here Might Not Get You There

Although leaders need to have a constant eye on their legacy, they must also be aware that their own skills need to change. Not simply impatient investors or unpredictable markets spell the end for leaders. In many companies, ambitious executives walk a knife's edge between healthy drive and destructive behaviors that can ruin their careers.

The Center for Creative Leadership in Greensboro, North Carolina, has been researching career derailment since 1983. Its findings suggest that each year as many as half of all high-flying executive careers derail: The executive gets fired, is demoted, or reaches a career plateau. Typically, these are people who have been placed on a fast trajectory to the top. Two of the main derailment factors are the inability or unwillingness to change or adapt and problems with interpersonal relationships.

Other studies have examined why some high-flyers suddenly experience a catastrophic reversal in their career progress, in some cases accompanied by psychological trauma. They suggest that a manager's perceived strengths often contribute to his or her downfall. What appear to be positive characteristics early in an individual's career can also have a dark side—for example, taking on multiple roles and responsibilities or volunteering to assist colleagues can lead to taking on too much.

Succession Planning

What is strange about the job of any leader is that the leader has an obligation to nurture a successor. The final element that should be in the top job's job description is one of the most neglected: succession planning.

"I've demanded of the top 20 people or so in the organization that they all have two 'ready now' candidates to do their job," Jim Skinner of McDonald's told me. "Now, we know that one will always be more ready than the other, but the fact is, the process of talent management, talent reviews, individual development programs, and the selection of high potentials has to yield people that are capable of doing a better job than the incumbent. If we're not doing that, we're not focused on continuous improvement, we're not picking the right high potentials, and we're not developing our people appropriately." Skinner and COO Ralph Alvarez regularly review the top 100 or so people in the organization to keep abreast of who's ready, how their development is going, and what further development is needed.

According to academics Warren Bennis and James O'Toole, getting leadership succession right requires boards to do the following:

1. Come to a shared definition of leadership
2. Resolve strategic and political conflicts
3. Actively measure the soft qualities in candidates
4. Beware of candidates who act like leaders, to avoid being seduced by charisma
5. Recognize that real leaders are threatening—the safe choice may be the wrong choice
6. Know that insider heirs usually aren't apparent—crown princes should be vetted with the same rigor as outsiders
7. Avoid rushing to judgment

"Part of good board governance is making good plans and identifying candidates for succession," one CEO told me. "I've been CEO for 11 years, and that's long enough. It's a stressful job, but getting the board involved with the succession process is not an easy task, either.

First of all, the CEO has to get him- or herself mentally prepared—but then you've got to engage your board in it."

This particular CEO spent four years on the succession process. "We asked ourselves what the next CEO in this changing business environment should be like. What sorts of skills or competences should he or she have? Even though you know you're not going to get all of these competences in one candidate, nevertheless, you should be able to identify what you want. We got into skills sets, and we got into innate qualities that you can't train for. We talked about language skills—should the next CEO in a global society have multiple-language capability? We talked about the global mind-set and those sorts of things."

The process also identified some innate qualities that could not be trained, including leadership style. "If you think about a leader who identifies with external or internal stakeholders, we wanted a CEO to have probably a little bit more external stakeholder focus than internal," says the CEO. "We even talked about the spouses and their role in the organization. We thought we needed a corporate cheerleader in the organization, someone to meet the press and be constantly involved with big customers. That's all style of leadership—that's not education or basic skills sets."

The End Is the Beginning

Top jobs change things. Indeed, change is the vital agenda of leadership. But top jobs also change the individual. A top job will change you. You will be tried and tested as never before. You will be pushed further than you ever imagined possible. You will be pressured. You will often feel exhausted as you balance commitment upon commitment.

Truth be told, a top job isn't for everyone, but to lead any organization or group of people is always an opportunity and a privilege. Often it is also an immense pleasure. Make of it what you will because it is yours to make the most of. But do so with fun and respect.

Key Points

- The final ingredient is the future. Unlike virtually any other job, leaders have to manage their own succession. Great companies have great succession planning and leaders who have a constant eye on their own legacy to the organization.
- Leaders are never forever. They are stewards of values, stewards of reputation, and guardians of high performance.
- Seize the opportunities to help make the lives of your employees more productive and enjoyable: help them to love their work.

Resources

Bennis, Warren, and James O'Toole. "Don't Hire the Wrong CEO." *Harvard Business Review* 78 (2000): 170–177.

Galford, Robert, and Maruca Regina Fazio. *Your Leadership Legacy* (Boston: Harvard Business School Press, 2006).

McCauley, Cynthia D., Russ S. Moxley, and Ellen Van Velsor (eds.). *The Center for Creative Leadership Handbook of Leadership Development* (San Francisco: Jossey-Bass, 1998).

Rothwell, William J. *Effective Succession Planning* (New York: Amacom, 2005).

Sims, Doris. *Building Tomorrow's Talent* (Bloomington: Authorhouse, 2007).

FINANCIAL TIMES

In an increasingly competitive world, it is quality
of thinking that gives an edge—an idea that opens new
doors, a technique that solves a problem, or an insight
that simply helps make sense of it all.

We work with leading authors in the various arenas
of business and finance to bring cutting-edge thinking
and best-learning practices to a global market.

It is our goal to create world-class print publications
and electronic products that give readers
knowledge and understanding that can then be
applied, whether studying or at work.

To find out more about our business
products, you can visit us at www.ftpress.com.

Your online source for premier business content

Safari Business Books Online provide electronic reference library for business professionals. With access to the thousands of books in the Safari library, you can easily find the answers you need to in a matter of seconds.

Some of Safari's features include:

- Review pre-published manuscripts for emerging business topics, before they are publicly available.

- Brush up on critical business skills by browsing across more than 30 categories of books, including business management, personal development, economics, and investing

- Gain exclusive access to the collections of FT Press, Wharton School Publishing, John Wiley and Sons, and Microsoft Press

- Access information on Safari when and where you need it, in realtime

Contact sales@safaribooksonline.com or call 888-619-1684 for Free Trial Offers and Enterprise Subscription Pricing.